On Mission in Mexico:

A Layman's Guide

James L. Lamar, Jr.

December 2008

ISBN 978-0-578-00389-4

Copyright © 2008, Jim Lamar, Santa Fe, Texas

All rights reserved

Dedicated to my wife Carol
and our daughters, Joy and Amanda,
for their unfailing support and encouragement.

Keep pushing me.
When I want it the least
is when I need it the most.

And in loving memory of
Hermano Marcelo Garcia,
who shared with us the joy
of working in Mexico missions
before he went home to be with the Lord.

Contents

Introduction	1
Chapter 1: How it all began	3
Chapter 2: Vicente Guerrero	9
Chapter 3: Galveston Baptist Association	21
Chapter 4: Diez y Seis de Septiembre	33
Chapter 5: GBA Recon II	51
Chapter 6: GBA Follow-up Trips 2003	57
Chapter 7: Faja de Oro	69
Chapter 8: El Limonál	93
Chapter 9: "Typical" mission trip itineraries	99
Chapter 10: Working in Mexico	105
PASSPORTS & TRAVEL VISAS	105
VEHICLE PERMITS	106
DRIVING IN MEXICO	108
TAKING MINORS	110
KEEPING IN TOUCH	111
MONEY EXCHANGE ISSUES	112
PERSONAL AND TEAM SUPPLIES	112
BORDER CROSSING DON'TS	114
Chapter 11: Cultural tips	117
Chapter 12: Summary and conclusions	123

Introduction

Growing up and living in Texas, my wife and I have had ample opportunity to interact with the Hispanic culture. Fifteen years ago (1993) these interactions led to our participation in a week long mission trip to Mexico. That trip was okay and we were pleased that God would allow us to be part of that effort, but no long term changes were made in our lives as a result of that trip. But in the year 2000 we became involved in a local Hispanic mission that was to change the way we saw missions forever. Over the course of the last eight years, from 2001 to 2008, we have been involved in many Mexico mission efforts and have seen hundreds of people come to a saving knowledge of Jesus Christ as a result.

This book is intended to share with you the trials, the victories, the pain and the pleasure of the mission journeys that we have been blessed to be a part of. More than just the documenting of historical events, our goal is to also provide a practical guide to others who may be hearing the call of the Father to go to this particular portion of the "uttermost parts of the world."

When you decide to answer the call to spread the gospel in Mexico, you are making a decision that will challenge you in ways in which you have never been challenged before. Crossing the border is not too difficult if you are staying within just a few miles of the border in what the Mexican government calls *la Frontera*, the Frontier. If you are called deeper into the interior than just a few short miles, the rules get a lot tougher. By the way, according to some estimates, over 80% of the mission work in Mexico takes place within 20 miles of the border. The dangers and difficulties of traveling into the interior prevent the majority of the work from affecting the majority of the Mexican populace. The language barrier is the first obvious difficulty to plan for, but did you know that to cross the frontier you also have to have travel visas for each person as well as a vehicle permit? Did you know that you will be stopped and questioned along the way regarding your destination, purpose, and length of stay?

The Lord has taught us many things during the last 8 years, and what we hope to do is to pass our learnings on to you in the hope that it will encourage you, educate you, and smooth out the wrinkles in the road you choose to follow. The road before you may look similar to the one we have traveled, or the Lord may have something completely different in store for you, but perhaps you can pick up something of value within these pages.

On Mission in Mexico

We will present a chronological history of the mission efforts that we have been involved with, as well as some very practical guidelines for crossing the border, crossing *la frontera*, packing for a stay in Mexico, and travel tips. We also have some practical information regarding cultural differences between the American and Mexican cultures that you will find very useful, regardless of how far you sojourn into Mexico.

As we provide the practical nuts and bolts of travel into Mexico, we also want to share with you some of the spiritual lessons that we learned along the way, again in the hopes that our learnings will help and encourage you.

The harvest is truly plentiful. Are you ready to be a harvester?

Jim & Carol Lamar
December 2008

Chapter 1: How it all began

There is so much to say, one must ask the age old question, "Where do I start?" The answer is, as usual, "At the beginning!" I was born in a small town in Pushmataha County, Oklahoma . . . okay; maybe that's just a little too far back! Let's go back to the late 1970's when Carol and I were students at Bee County College. Carol was the president of the Baptist Student Union. I was one of the guys. One of our BSU projects was a bike-a-thon to raise money for summer missionaries. As Carol and I got in shape for this bike-a-thon we spent a lot of time riding our bikes around town and out to neighboring towns. We got to know each other pretty well. I was envious of her ability to play the guitar and sing, and during this time she taught me to play a few chords on a guitar that was always left lying around the Baptist Student Center.

After Jr. College we went our own ways for a few years, Carol to Howard Payne University and me to Texas A&I University. While a student at A&I God blessed me with a wonderful Christian roommate named Paul Rodriquez. He happened to be a Catholic, but neither of us let denominational boundaries get in the way of our faith. He often attended services with me at Calvary Baptist Church in Kingsville on Sundays. For nearly a year he allowed me to play guitar and sing with him and the choir at the Catholic Student Union on Sunday afternoons when Mass was held for the students. Many of the choir members at the CSU were also spirit filled Christians. On Friday nights Lt. Colonel Melendez, Commander for the A&I ROTC post, hosted a Bible study in his home. Every Bible study included a time of prayer and a time of singing and fellowship. Even though I was just learning to play, these folks allowed me to bring my guitar and try to keep up, which is about all I could do! What God did for me during these three years was provide me with willing teachers and patient audiences such that I learned to play the guitar well enough to accompany myself or others if they were willing to take the chance. One of the other students at the BSU was Feliz. She had already given her life to missions and felt like she needed to learn to play the guitar and take one with her onto the mission field. I was just a beginner myself but ended up teaching her what little I knew to get her started.

During Carol's time at Bee County College and again at Howard Payne University, she spent her summers working as a summer missionary in the Rio Grande River Ministry program, run by the Baptist General Convention of Texas. Before we ever got serious about each other, she was serious about mission work along the Rio Grande. If you want to strike up an interesting

On Mission in Mexico

conversation with her, ask her about her experiences as a summer missionary some time!

Carol and I reconnected during my third (and last) year at A&I, while she was teaching school at Lamar Elementary in Sinton, and ended up getting married two days after my graduation in 1982. Off we went to West Virginia to start my career as a Chemical Engineer. We joking tell people now that we were missionaries to the hillbillies of West Virginia, but in fact we were pretty much consumed with starting our family and my career, both of our daughters being born during this time. Eventually we were able to secure a transfer back home; leaving "Almost Heaven" in early 1990 for what we think is the closest thing to heaven on earth – Texas.

As I mentioned in the Introduction, we participated in a mission trip to Tampico, Mexico in 1993, but did not see this trip as a life changing experience. If we could have seen ahead we would have known differently. God was continuing his preparations unbeknownst to us.

Sometime in the late 1990's our church, Pine Drive Baptist in Dickinson, made the decision to help a fledgling Hispanic mission. Since both Carol and I spoke a spattering of Spanish we were asked to serve on the Missions Committee and help out as liaisons to this small mission. Initially, the mission was meeting in the Pine Drive fellowship hall. The pastor of this mission, Hermano Marcelo Garcia, was a jovial fellow whom we would come to love as a brother in the years to follow. Somewhere in the beginnings of our relationship with him he asked me to sing a song at the mission which I did. Not long after that he asked me if I could teach him to play the guitar. Since I had a little experience teaching basic guitar before, I agreed. The Lord taught me a lesson then about leaning on my own understanding. As it turns out the Spanish song books do not use the same musical alphabet that we use. Our musical alphabet consists of the notes A, B, C, D, E, F, and G. The Spanish musical alphabet consists of the notes Do, Re, Mi, Fa, So, La, and Ti. To make things more interesting, A does not map to Do and B does not map to Re. It took a little

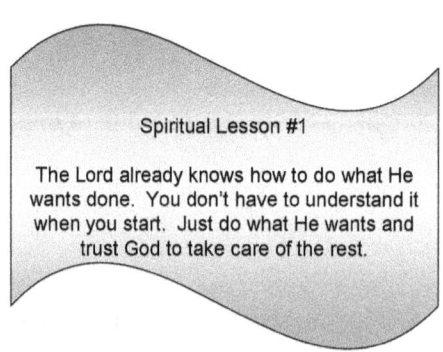

Spiritual Lesson #1

The Lord already knows how to do what He wants done. You don't have to understand it when you start. Just do what He wants and trust God to take care of the rest.

investigation to find out that the Spanish musical alphabet starts with the English note C. After this great revelation I created a Spanish version of my guitar class so that I could be musically bilingual.

During the course of these guitar lessons we became good friends with Hermano Marcelo, his wife Maria, and many members of their small congregation. Some of their number were originally from Mexico and still had family south of the border. In 2001 these folks invited us to go with them on a week long mission trip to Cuidad Mante, about 300 miles south of Brownsville. Carol would help out in Vacation Bible School and I would play the guitar and sing. Hermano Marcelo was a member of the Galveston Baptist Association (GBA) Missions Committee. Upon our return from this mission trip he asked me to accompany him to the next committee meeting. That meeting led to a greater involvement in Mexico missions by the GBA and the adoption of a resolution that the GBA would concentrate on Mexico missions for a period of three years. This led to many more mission trips by many people from many churches.

In January of 2002 several of us went back to Mexico, but not to conduct Vacation Bible School. The goal of this trip was to meet with pastors from the Mexican Baptist churches in the area to see if there were opportunities to have our groups work together for the Lord. In July of 2002 the GBA sponsored a mission effort that sent 5 teams of people to Mexico made up of 59 people from 9 local churches. In February of 2003 the Executive Director of the GBA traveled with a group of us back to Mexico to discuss the results of this effort with the director of the Mexican Baptist Association. In July 2003 four more teams of people from the GBA were sent to Mexico. This work continued throughout 2004 and 2005. Even with the termination of the 3 year concentration on Mexico missions by the GBA, the work continues to move forward, as God knew it would.

We have record of hundreds of people in Mexico that have come to a saving knowledge of Jesus Christ in the last few years because of these mission efforts. There are surely more that we do not know about, but that's okay. God knows each one by name and has recorded every name in the Lamb's book of life. Some of these new Christians came to

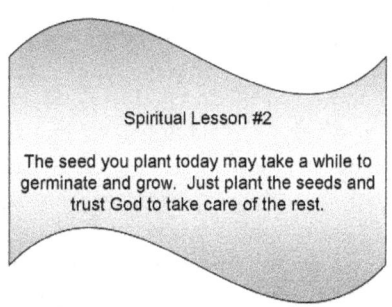

Spiritual Lesson #2

The seed you plant today may take a while to germinate and grow. Just plant the seeds and trust God to take care of the rest.

know Jesus because they heard the gospel during one of our mission trips. Our involvement in these mission trips took place because of the relationship we forged with Hermano Marcelo while teaching him to play the guitar, which I could only do because Carol taught me to play over 20 years ago.

Mexico's official name is Los Estados Unidos Mexicanos

Our work was mostly in the state of Tamaulipas working with the Bethsaida Baptist Association. Our efforts were centered in Ciudad Mante, Located approximately 350 miles south of Harlingen, Texas.

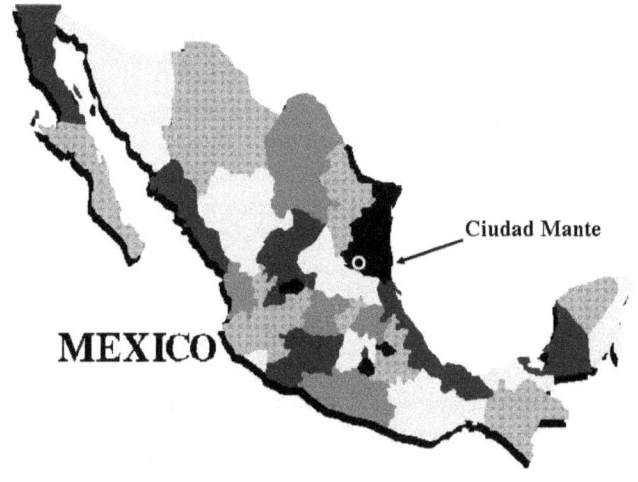

A member of Arcadia First Baptist Church donated a guitar to the mission effort. We left it in the hands of one of the missions down there. Two years later we find a teenaged girl named Sulema playing the guitar and singing praises in church. She even learned how to sing "Here I Am to Worship" in English for us so we could worship with her. So the snowball continues to roll. Who knows how many people will come to know the Lord in the years to come because of this young lady's ministry which all started with a donated guitar?

The man who donated the guitar did not accompany us on the trip and to my knowledge has never met Sulema, yet he played a key role in kicking off her ministry south of the border. Others in our congregation have donated money to help defer expenses of the trip. They too are a part of every salvation experience and every success. Still others are prayer warriors, holding the missions teams up before the throne while we travel. Each member of the body has its own function, and none of us would function well without the other members. Sounds kind of scriptural, doesn't it? I like to think of it like this: whether you pray, or go, or provide, you are part of the team. Part of the team is the home team, providing fiscal and prayer support. Part of the team is the field team, taking the word out to the mission field. Only by working together do we accomplish what God lays before us.

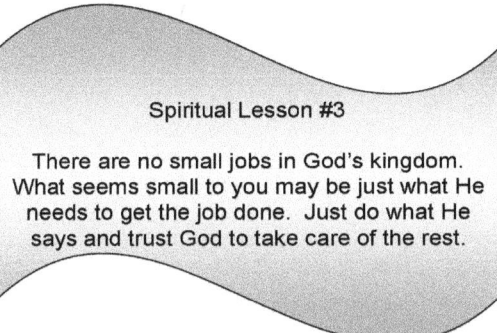

Spiritual Lesson #3

There are no small jobs in God's kingdom. What seems small to you may be just what He needs to get the job done. Just do what He says and trust God to take care of the rest.

I have often wondered what ever happened to Feliz and the mission service to which she was called. In the case of Sulema singing praises in a little mission in Mexico, Carol can see the results of her teaching me to play the guitar. In other cases, such as Feliz, we may not know the results on this side of the Jordan. Either way, it's all in God's hands.

Chapter 2: Vicente Guerrero

Now that we've provided an overall outline of what has happened over the last few years, let's fill in some details and show you some pictures to help you better understand the nature of a mission trip to Mexico. Hermano Marcelo was the pastor of Primera Iglésia Bautista (Spanish for First Church Baptist), a mission of Pine Drive Baptist Church in Dickinson, Texas. He had contacts with folks in a local church in the town of Ciudad Mante in the southern part of the Mexican state of Tamaulipas, about 300 miles south of Brownsville. In Cd. Mante are a couple of Baptist churches, one of them called Iglésia Bautista Emmanuel. This little Mexican Baptist church had a very active youth group that was working in a suburb, they call it a colónia, called Vicente Guerrero. Vicente Guerrero had no church of any kind. Many people think that Mexico is completely catholic and that it would be futile for evangelicals to attempt to spread the gospel there. This is not the case. It is true that there are Catholic churches in all of the larger cities and that Catholicism is the only sanctioned church in Mexico, but we have yet to see a Catholic church outside of the larger cities. The majority of Mexicans live in suburbs (colónias) or government sponsored villages (ejidos) and do not have access to a church of any kind. The work we were asked to undertake was to join forces with the youth of Iglésia Emmanuel as God had already directed them to start a mission in Vicente Guerrero. If you are familiar with the Experiencing God study by Henry Blackaby will recognize this spiritual truth. Look around, see where God is at work around you, and then join Him. So we did.

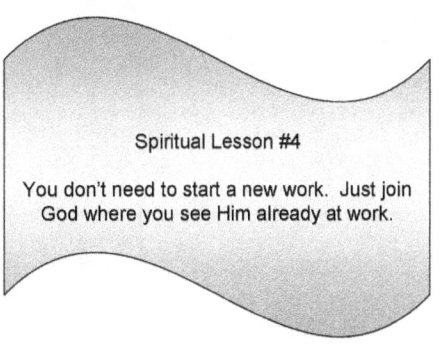

Spiritual Lesson #4

You don't need to start a new work. Just join God where you see Him already at work.

Off we went then, twelve adults and a couple of younger kids to work with the youth of Iglésia Bautista Emmanuel in the colónia of Vicente Guerrero. We left Dickinson at about 2:00 AM so we could arrive at the border, nearly 300 miles south of us, about the time the immigration office opened. Being our first trip with this group we really didn't know what to expect. Sitting around the border offices for several hours to obtain the necessary travel visas and permits was not what we expected, but as it turns out is completely normal. In the years to follow we would learn that a quick and efficient border crossing is the exception, not the rule. In Chapter 10 we'll share some very useful information to help you make the crossing as efficiently as possible. (That's me in the

On Mission in Mexico

cowboy hat and Carol standing in front of me. Hermano Marcelo is beside me, second from the left on the back row.)

The July 2001 Mission team from Primera Iglésia Bautista in Dickinson, Texas

After obtaining our personal visas and vehicle permits we make our way south of the border. Due to the poor road conditions it takes nearly 8 more hours to make the 300 mile drive from the border to Cd. Mante, but we make the entire trip in one day, arriving late Saturday evening. Somewhere along the way we pass a sign on the side of the road that said we were crossing the Tropic of Cancer. On Sunday morning we attend church at Iglésia Emmanuel and meet the youth who are working on this mission. After lunch we all take the 20 minute drive out to Vicente Guerrero to begin canvassing the streets, inviting folks to VBS. (In Spanish Vacation Bible School is Escuela Biblia de Vacaciones or EBDV) Picture the scene in your mind. We are hundreds of miles south of the border, in the tropics, in July. The temperature on Sunday afternoon is well over 100 degrees Fahrenheit and we're walking up and down the dirt streets of this little colónia letting the locals know that there will be VBS meetings in the mornings and services in the evenings of the upcoming week. Many of the Mexican ladies are still very conservative when it comes to the appropriate attire for church related activities, so all of our female team members are in dresses or skirts. Some are even in heels, making navigation of the rough, unpaved streets even more interesting.

With our new friend, Adriana, we walk the dirt streets of Vicente Guerrero on Sunday afternoon.

We have many more cultural hints to offer in Chapter 11, but one of the first things we learned about the Mexican culture on this trip happened during this Sunday walk through the town. It is very hot and we are conducting this walk through in the middle of the day. Many of the people who live in these colónias are not very well off. There homes are relatively small affairs and absolutely nobody around there has air conditioning. Many of the houses are little more than places to sleep with a kitchenette attached. The coolest place to be in the heat of the day is outside underneath a shade tree. As we walk around we see that most people are sitting around in the front yard talking or playing dominoes. Most of the yards are fenced in. In the United States we would be accustomed to walking through the gate to greet the people. In Mexico this would be the equivalent of walking directly into their living room, so you just don't do it. Instead, you stand at the gate and shout a greeting of "buenas tardes" or good afternoon. They may respond; they may not. If they do respond you ask them for permission to speak to them and for a minute of their time. Again they may allow this or they may say that they are too busy. Only when given permission would you walk through the gate to talk to them and pass out a flyer with information regarding the upcoming services. We learn a valuable lesson about the need to respect the cultural norms of the people we

On Mission in Mexico

are visiting and the absolute necessity to partner with the locals who understand this culture intimately. Otherwise, our cause is lost before we ever get started.

Through the connections of one of the locals, we have permission to use a vacant lot in Vicente Guerrero for the Vacation Bible School and evening services. There is no building. There is no running water. There are no facilities; just a vacant lot with a gorgeous collection of avocado, banana, and orange trees. We haul in some plastic chairs from the host church, hang a few tarps up to provide some additional shade, and put out balloons and streamers to draw attention to the location. Come Monday morning, we set out to conduct VBS just as if there were no challenges at all to our circumstances.

Opening Assembly on Monday

We hold an opening assembly just like we would here in the states. There is singing, and pledges to the Mexican flag, the Christian flag, and the Bible. Over 50 kids show up to start off our week. By the end of the week we have nearly 100 kids showing up for VBS every morning and over a dozen adults! The crowd is broken up by age group and classes begin. We don't have any class rooms so the different groups just fan out across the property wherever they can find a shady spot. The youth from Iglésia Emmanuel teach some of the classes; Hermano Marcelo teaches the youth and adult class. Other members of our party work on providing a time to work on crafts and we have the different age groups rotate through the craft area. The adults there really get into the craft time. We also provide refreshments, consisting of a punch drink and cookies.

VBS: The 8 to 11 year olds

Another cultural difference is revealed to us. These folks start things when they think it is time to start things. The flyer said VBS would start at 9:00 AM. In Mexico this is more of a suggestion than a hard and fast plan. You might interpret this time as being, "we will start sometime after 9:00 AM when everything is ready." The same thing goes for quitting time. I actually like this part. They quit when they're finished and not a minute before. If the preacher isn't finished delivering the message he believes God wants delivered until 1:00 PM, then he preaches until 1:00 PM. If the congregational participation in the service through multiple special music presentations and 30 minutes of testimonies causes the service to go overtime, nobody cares. Nobody is watching the clock. VBS works that way as well. We planned to conduct VBS from 9:00 AM to Noon, but rarely wrapped up until 12:30 or 1:00 PM. Lunch in the afternoon was a laid back affair at the host church provided by the ladies of Iglésia Emmanuel. We had a few hours in the late afternoon to visit the local market or (more commonly) take a nap in the cool confines of our hotel rooms. Often times the afternoon hours were used to prepare the lessons and crafts for the next day's VBS. Later in the evening we conducted revival services back in Vicente Guerrero. Naturally we had to return to the scene early in order to

On Mission in Mexico

rearrange the available furniture and have everything prepped and ready to go. Revival services down there are just like the ones we conduct north of the border. They have an opening prayer, sing a few songs, usually have special music presented, then there is a time of preaching. The difference is that down there the services were conducted outside, in 90 plus degree heat, in plastic chairs, under huge fruit trees, and last 2 hours.

Jim & Ruben sing at the evening service under the avocado tree.

Hermano Marcelo prays as he prepares to deliver the message.

During the course of this week long adventure we got my custom van stuck in the mud after an afternoon thunderstorm. We also experienced what seemed like a devastating flat when the side wall of one tire on the van was punctured. In the U.S. you can't fix a flat that involves a severely punctured sidewall. In Mexico they fixed it in an hour and I happen to know that that repaired tire is still on the van and still holding up just fine **7 years later**. It got hot. We got tired. We got cranky. We persevered. By the end of the week we counted 29 children and 18 adults as new members of the family of God. The Father allowed us to see a bountiful harvest in that trip, making sure we would forget all about the trials and the tires and the heat, remembering only the joy of seeing Him at work and allowing us to be a part of it.

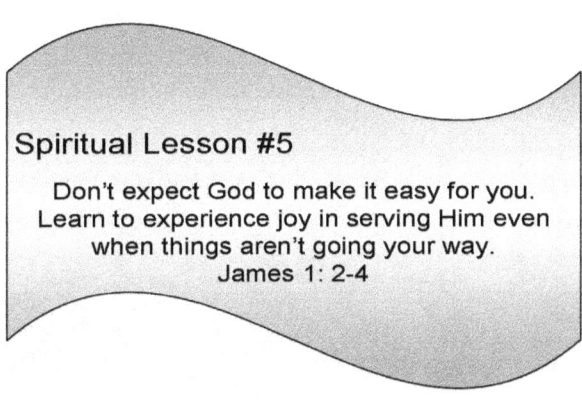

Spiritual Lesson #5

Don't expect God to make it easy for you. Learn to experience joy in serving Him even when things aren't going your way.
James 1: 2-4

The trip home was relatively uneventful as nothing the world could throw at us could discourage us after seeing God working so mightily that week. In the next chapter I'll pick up the story of what happened back home following this trip, but I didn't want to leave you hanging regarding how the mission work in Vicente Guerrero turns out. As Paul Harvey would say, here is "the rest of the story."

On Mission in Mexico

The Rest of the Story

After our mission efforts in July 0f 2001, the owner of the vacant lot decided to donate half of that lot to the community for a church. With his generous donation the host church (Iglésia Emmanuel) got started on the building project. Several of us returned to Vicente Guerrero in January of 2002 to check on their progress and found them busily digging the foundation, by hand. Heavy equipment is expensive but labor is CHEAP in Mexico.

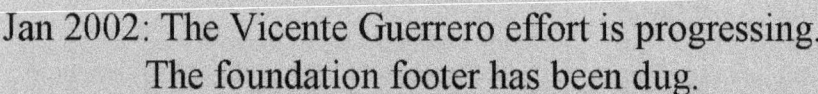

Jan 2002: The Vicente Guerrero effort is progressing. The foundation footer has been dug.

By the time we returned in July of 2002 they had completed the floor and 3 walls of the building. Services were held "indoors" that summer for the first time – loosely speaking. In February of 2003 we had to meet outside again because the 4th wall was finished and the roof was under construction.

Vicente Guerrero

July 2002: The Mission at Vicente Guerrero now has 3 walls.
(and a tarp full of water)
Money was left to finish the front wall and the roof.

As of Feb 2003 Vicente Guerrero has 4 walls and
are building the forms for the roof.

In July of 2003 the mission has a concrete roof and is officially open for business. That summer marked the first time the mission could truly meet indoors.

July 2003: The front of the Vicente Guerrero mission – it still needs doors and windows

Finally in July 2004 we see the finished product: Mision Bautista Peniel.

The mission in Vicente Guerrero is filled to capacity on Sundays in 2004. The Medical Mission took place here.

The mission trip of July 2004 was a very interesting one. By then we had so many teams going into Mexico that our groups were split up and working in several different little towns. The group that Carol and I were working with was in a little village 30 minutes outside of Cd. Mante, but we were staying in the same hotel as the group working in Vicente Guerrero. The two teams combined their efforts for a major medical mission at Vicente Guerrero on Sunday before we started our respective Vacation Bible School efforts. Hermano Arturo presented the gospel to those waiting to see the Doctor using a neat little gadget called an Evangicube. This thing tells the gospel story in pictures and when used properly is a very effective witnessing tool. We saw another 25 souls added to God's kingdom on that day alone.

Hermano Arturo presents the gospel using an Evangicube during our one day medical mission.

With the mission at Vicente Guerrero completed and filling to capacity nearly every Sunday, the Texas based missions teams turned their attentions to other opportunities. We still enjoy stopping in to visit these old friends from time to time when we are down there working nearby.

Chapter 3: Galveston Baptist Association

Upon our return from the mission trip to Vicente Guerrero in July of 2001, we immediately began making plans to return in 2002. We were very excited to be a part of what God was doing in Mexico and were not shy about telling people about our trip. At that time, Hermano Marcelo was serving on the Missions Committee for the Galveston Baptist Association (GBA) so naturally the committee heard all about the trip. Wanting some help with telling the story, he asked me to come to a couple of committee meetings with him and before I knew what hit me, I was a member. We put together a PowerPoint presentation about our trip and shared this information with the association at large, along with a committee recommendation to adopt the Bethsaida Baptist Convention (responsible for the portion of Mexico wherein we were working), Seattle, and the Kankanay people of the Philippines as our three focused mission thrusts for the next three years. This recommendation was approved by the GBA in October of 2001.

Based on the support of the GBA to get more involved in Mexico missions, we took a small team of 8 folks from 3 different GBA churches back to Cd. Mante in January of 2002 to ask them where else God was working and how might we be a part of those efforts.

We met with about a dozen pastors from all over the Bethsaida Baptist Association as well as the associational Missions Director. From this meeting we choose several places to visit personally.

Again, we were not looking to start any thing new. We were just to looking to see where God was at work around us. When that meeting concluded, pastors from the local association down there were lined up to have us come see the opportunities at their church. We spent the rest of our time in Mexico traveling to the various churches that expressed an interest in partnering with us and collecting data.

By the end of our trip we had developed a list of 10 churches that desired our help and participation. The names of the missions or churches are provided here followed by the name of the town. If the town is too small to provide hotel services for our visiting mission teams I've included the name of the larger town that might provide such services in parentheses.

1. Misión Vicente Guerrero – Ciudád Mante
2. Misión Santa Júlia – Aldama
3. Iglésia Monte Horeb – EJ 16 de Septembre (Ciudád Mante)
4. Iglésia Emmanuel – Tampico *(not visited)*
5. Misión Chamesál – Ciudád Victória
6. Misión Carrera Torres – Aldama
7. Iglésia Bautista Betél – Cuauhtemoc
8. Misión El Buen Samaritán – Colónia Progresso (Ciudád Mante)
9. Primera Iglésia Bautista – Limón *(not visited)*
10. Principe de Paz – Guemez

First on our list of potential places to minister was of course the mission in Vicente Guerrero where some of us had already been working. Since the entire previous chapter was devoted to discussion of the efforts at that location, we won't go over that information again.

Next on our priority list was a little mission called Santa Julia outside of the town of Aldama, about 2 hours away from Ciudad Mante. Hosted by Primera Iglésia Bautista Aldama, this mission was running about 12 adults and 15 children on Sundays. Their desire was for help in putting on Vacation Bible School. The pictures we have are of the thatched roof hut where they were meeting at the time. One member of their small congregation had already donated a corner lot in where they could build their own church building and the congregation had already collected sufficient funds to prepare the foundation. They expected to have the foundation completed before we could return in July.

The Mission at Santa Julia. Here's where they currently meet

Pastor Silva shows hermano German the bench that constitutes the adult Sunday School department facility.

Number three on the list was Iglésia Monte Horeb in the ejido of 16 de Septembre, about 20 minutes outside of Ciudád Mante. Pastor Rudulfo Leal specifically requested a mixed team of Anglos and Hispanics. It seems in these little rural areas, Anglo visitors are something of a rarity.

Ejido 16th de Septembre
Iglésia Monte Horeb

They had a church and were Struggling to add on a couple of Sunday School classrooms.

It also struck me that this church asks more for spiritual support than they did fiscal support. It seemed that their little church was struggling with what amounted to spiritual depression and was looking for revival.

Unlike many of the places we visited, this was a fully constituted church, not a mission, and they already had a building in which to meet. They had even been in the process of adding on a couple of Sunday School rooms, but that effort had somewhat stalled. This particular opportunity struck a chord with me for some reason so Carol and I ended up working on the mission team that chose this church as our project. More details about what we did and how it went will thus be shared in the next chapter. (It's good news.)

There were a couple of mission opportunities that we ended up putting on our priority list but that we did not get time to visit in person. Number four on our list falls into this category. Iglésia Emmanuel in Tampico had land, but no building. They were averaging 30 in attendance meeting in a house outside of town that was not big enough to hold them all, with a layman as their preacher. They were asking for help with Vacation Bible School as well as revival services in July, and for help with a future construction project on their piece of land.

Next on our list was Misión Chamesál outside of Ciudad Victoria, sponsored by Iglésia Betél. As you can see in the picture below, these folks were meeting under a pole barn type shed with a tin roof and no walls. At the time they were running 10 to 15 adults and 15 children on Sundays. The mission work here was being directed by a couple of ladies from the host church.

They obviously had many physical needs, such as walls, doors, running water, and electricity, but what they requested was Vacation Bible School and revival services. They said there were over 50 families within walking distance and that we could reasonably expect 75 to 80 children in VBS if we would come.

This is the mission at Chamesal - outside of Ciudad Victoria.

On Mission in Mexico

Coming in at number six on our list was a new mission work at Carrerra Torres, also outside of Aldama.

One of our stops is the home of Cristina Lopez Maldanado in EJ Carrera Torres. Pastor Silva introduces us. She holds Church here every Sunday with 20+ people attending.

From the back of the house you can see just how it is built.

Our seventh priority opportunity was Iglésia Bautista Betél in Cuauhtemoc, located about an hour from Aldama and two hours from Cd. Mante.

Saul leads the way toward Iglesia Bautista Betel in Cuauhtemoc. About an hour from Aldama and two hours from Ciudad Mante.

The main need expressed here was for spiritual awakening and renewal. They wanted help with VBS and Revival services and have a great auditorium for showing the Jesus video. Since their need is spiritual a prayer team would also be appropriate - but then, when is a prayer team inappropriate?

The pastor's name is Andres Gonzalez. He offered his people to assist with food preparation in the church kitchen as a mechanism to keep travel costs for the team at a minimum. We noticed that their Sunday School class rooms and the bathrooms were in need of doors, windows, and paint, but a construction crew was not specifically requested.

This facility, unlike many of the rural places we visited, was in a fairly congested area with a very large potential audience. We were told that you could expect 80 – 100 children in VBS. At that time they were running 25 children and 25 adults on Sundays.

On Mission in Mexico

Next up was Misión El Buen Samaritán in Colónia Progresso, also on the outskirts of Cd. Mante.

El Buen Samaritan. Not fancy, but very snug.

Deacon Jose Luis Maldanado (shown with Brother Marcelo) is hoping to build a 4 x 8 meter room back here as a parsonage for a full time pastor, maybe a recent seminary graduate.

Number nine on our list was Primera Iglésia Bautista Limón. This mission, located just minutes away from Cd. Mante asked only for a prayer team. Because of their request, we did not take time to visit them on location. The pastor at this mission asked only that we pray for them from our homes in Texas and if possible, send a team people to walk the streets and pray for them in Mexico. His comments reminded me of the commander with the sick daughter that told Jesus that a personal visit wasn't necessary, just command her to be well and she will be.

Rounding out our top ten opportunities was the church Principe de Paz (it means Prince of Peace) in Guemez. This new church was already under construction right on the town square in Guemez, directly across the plaza from the Catholic Church. The walls were up and a small portion of the front of the building is roofed and has lights so they can hold services there now. They need doors, widows, a roof, etc. Due to the size of this place it could not be completed in a single visit. It would need to be completed in stages over several years.

At that time they had approximately 70 people meeting there. The growth opportunity was tremendous due to its location and the town of over 2,000 that is built around it. A deacon named José Martinez handles the preaching. Principe de Paz in Ciudád Victória is the sponsoring church.

Located on the town square in Guemez is Iglesia Principe de Paz , obviously still under construction.

They've completed just enough of the front portion to begin using the facility for church. They run 70 people on Sundays.

For the GBA we organized all of this information into a PowerPoint presentation with pictures and information about each one of these opportunities, including details such as costs of construction, expected numbers of VBS participants, etc. as appropriate. Once again we brought the opportunities before the association and asked them to state their pleasure. The local pastors responded with enthusiasm and excitement.

One of the things that we noted in our presentation to the association was that if every church in the GBA would donate $1 per day for the three year term of this mission emphasis, we could completely fund every single mission opportunity that we identified in this first recon trip. In Mexico, where labor is unbelievably cheap, a little bit of money goes a very long way.

Galveston Baptist Association

Mexico Mission Opportunity Grid

July 2002	Mission/Church Location Accommodations	Misión Vicente Guerrero Vicente Guerrero Ciudád Mante	Misión Santa Júlia Santa Júlia Aldama	Iglésia Monte Horeb EJ 16 de Septiembre Ciudád Mante	Misión Chamesái Chamesái Ciudád Victória	Misión Carrera T. Carrera Tor Aldam
	Priority	1	2	3	4	5
	Lead Church =>	Primera - Dickinson	Primera - Friendswood	Pine Drive - Dickinson	Oklahoma Crew	1st Baptist - Dickinson
	Helper Church =>	Rockview		Calvary - Tex City		Primera - Dickinson
Bi-lingual	VBS Teacher Primary					
	VBS Helper			C Lamar		
Bi-lingual	VBS Teacher Secondary					
	VBS Helper			D Weber		
Bi-lingual	VBS Teacher - Youth					
	VBS Helper					
Bi-lingual	Preacher					
	Music					
Bi-lingual	Translator					
Bi-lingual	Translator					
	Video			R Reyes		
	Video			J Lamar		
	Prayer Walk			J Groebner		
	Prayer Walk			Local		
	Other					
	Construction					
	Construction					
	Construction					
	Construction					
	Construction					
	Construction					
	Financial	$1,000		$1,000		
	Total Team Membership:	0	0	0	0	0
	Service Days:	M - Th	M - Th	Th		M - Th

We developed a spreadsheet to help organize the assembling of teams to minister in the various churches and missions where the needs had been identified and where we felt God was already at work. At first it seemed a little overwhelming to attempt to minister to all ten of these opportunities, but in His usual miraculous goodness, God brought forth contacts from other states of churches that were convicted of the need to minister in Mexico but did not know how nor where to begin. We folded them into the efforts God had placed before us and gave thanks for His provisions. It would not be possible to show the entire spreadsheet in a book of this format, but at least you can see a piece of the spreadsheet above.

It took several months to finalize the plans, but when we gathered as a group to head south in July of 2002, there were 59 people from the GBA representing 7 different churches organized into 5 teams. In addition, we had helped to coordinate two additional teams from out of state, and had assembled a video team. God had multiplied the initial mission effort by a factor of 5 in the just one year!

- Primera Iglésia Dickinson and Rockview Church were sent together to minister at Vicente Guerrerro.
- Primera Friendswood was sent to Misión Santa Julia in Aldama.
- Pine Drive Baptist Church Dickinson and Calvary Baptist Texas City were sent to Iglésia Monte Horeb in the ejido of 16 de Septiembre.
- A mission team from Oklahoma was directed to Chamesál in Ciudad Victoria.
- First Baptist Church Dickinson, supported with members of Primera Iglésia Dickinson, were sent o Misión Carrerra Torres in Aldama.
- A mission team from South Carolina was sent to Misión El Buen Samaritan in Colonia Progresso.
- Mt. Zion Baptist Church Texas City was sent to Iglésia Emmanuel in Tampico.
- Finally, a GBA video team was assembled in the hopes that we could at least show the Jesus video in the remaining churches and missions.

The effort to get the churches of the GBA more actively involved and participating in Mexico missions was led by the GBA Missions Committee, which was of course led by the Executive Director of Missions. That position was filled at the time by Dr. Kyle Cox. He wouldn't want it, so we won't praise him for his work, but we will praise God for his servant's heart and vision for missions.

Chapter 4: Diez y Seis de Septiembre

Based on what we had seen and how we felt the Spirit moving us, Carol and I were part of the Pine Drive Baptist Church team that traveled to 16 de Septiembre in July of 2002, loading up our vehicles at 2:00 AM so we could get to the border about the time they opened up to receive visitors.

Loading up to leave from Pine Drive at 2:00 AM . . .

It takes us 6 or 7 hours to reach the border but since most of the folks have cat napped a bit along the way, we're doing okay. The border crossing is sometimes a quick and easy thing to accomplish, but often times we spend hours trying to navigate the ever changing immigration rules. Once across, the trip down to Ciudad Mante is about the same number of miles, but takes even longer due to the road conditions. A major highway in Mexico is a two lane road with shoulders so slower traffic can pull to the right and allow faster traffic to pass. The shoulders are not really wide enough to make them a full driving lane. They may be ¾ of a car width so the passing vehicle still has to crowd across the center line. When you see cars passing both directions simultaneously, you really wish you weren't driving . . .

Border crossing

We stopped along the way at a scenic overlook

Diez y Seis de Septiembre

Finally we make it to our destination, and set up to conduct Vacation Bible School each morning and revival services each evening. Remember how the church building looked when we saw it in January of 2002?

Iglésia Monte Horeb, located in the EJ 16 de Septiembre, about 20 minutes from downtown Ciudad Mante. This is how it looked in January 2002.

On Mission in Mexico

By the time we returned in July they were well on their way to completion!

This is how it looked in July, 2002.
Two brand new Sunday School rooms - with a roof!

The good news was that they were making progress. The bad news was that the roof was so new that the concrete (yes – a concrete roof!) was not yet cured so we would not be able to use the new rooms during our visit that summer.

Diez y Seis de Septiembre

The roof is on but not cured enough to take down the forms so we had to hold VBS outside.
We left enough money to put in windows, doors, and a floor.

Instead, we held classes pretty much anywhere we could find or make a shady spot. In the pictures to follow you will see classes meeting in tents in the front yard of the church, under a lean-to that we could only use sometimes because of the mud caused by mid week rains, and even in the shadow of the church building itself in the morning hours.

The folks we were ministering to do not speak English so every class has to be led by one of the local church members or we have to provide translators to get the message across. On this trip we had a mixture of delivery styles.

Susan went with us as translator. She also taught the middle age group and ran 10 - 12 kids every day.

The phantom photographer - caught in the act!
This was the younger children's VBS class room.

Diez y Seis de Septiembre

Class rooms are where ever you can find some shade.
Some dogs just won't sit still for the lesson . . .

The youth class also ran about a dozen daily. In Mexico, the youth class is everybody over the age of 12.

On Mission in Mexico

One of the big draws in Mexico is the craft portion of Vacation Bible School. We have seen people in their 60's and 70's showing up for VBS so they could participate in the crafts.

Craft time goes over **BIG** in Mexico.

For this trip we took blank canvas bags and let the folks customize with their hand prints on one side and the Christian flag on the other. I still have mine, signed by nearly everybody that attended.

We would try to wrap things up shortly after noon, but as we've mentioned before, things rarely start on time and nobody is watching the clock too closely, so you finish when you finish. Our friends from Primera Iglésia Bautista Dickinson were still working in Vicente Guerrero and both teams were staying in the same motel in Ciudad Mante. Iglésia Emmanuel had offered to feed both mission teams lunch every day, so we were a little anxious to get back to town, but as with everything else, lunch was served when it was ready and this event didn't follow a rigid time schedule. We left 16 de Septiembre "late" several times but never once found ourselves late for lunch.

After lunch the team members have a few hours to relax in the air conditioned hotel or visit the market place (el Mercado) for a little local shopping. Many afternoons would find the team members practicing special music for the evening services or prepping their materials for VBS the next day.

Diez y Seis de Septiembre

After VBS we met up with the Primera Iglesia Dickinson group back at Iglesia Emanuel in Ciudad Mante for lunch.

In the evenings we gather back at the church for revival services.

Theresa sings "Via Dolorosa" for the evening service.
(Jim tries desperately to keep up)

On Mission in Mexico

In the evening, Steve preached and Susan interpreted

They ran fans to move the hot air around a little. It helped – a little.

The church building is located within feet of sheep pens. The noise and the smell were something new for us to deal with.

Diez y Seis de Septiembre

Right beside the church is a collection of sheep pens. Most evenings the shepherd would feel the need to feed his sheep while we were having services. The bawling of the sheep and the attack on our olfactory senses were something that we were not used to dealing with in the United States. It certainly provides you with an opportunity to practice your patience.

We worked and sweated all week long. We did what we thought we were called to do. At the end of the week we had not seen a single conversion. Not a single person had come forward to make a public profession of faith.

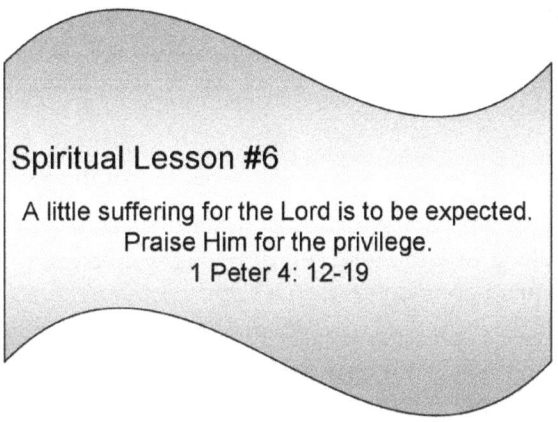

Spiritual Lesson #6

A little suffering for the Lord is to be expected. Praise Him for the privilege.
1 Peter 4: 12-19

A sign along the sign of the road between Ciudad Mante and 16 de Septembre reminds us of our purpose.

This sign on the road between 16 de Septiembre and Ciudad Mante declares that Jesus Christ is Lord of Ciudad Mante.

On Mission in Mexico

We finished up our work and headed back to Texas tired and wondering if we had made a difference. To make matters worse, the AC went out on my van as we were leaving Ciudad Mante. We made some switches to put the men in the hot van and allow the women to travel in the other vehicles in our convoy for the trip. We made it to within about 60 miles of home before the belt wore through and broke completely, stranding us in Needville, Texas. By the time we finally got a wrecker to pick up the van and get us all home, we were pretty much beaten down.

The Rest of the Story

It would be a sad state of affairs indeed if that was the end of the story for Iglésia Monte Horeb in 16 de Septiembre, but God was working in ways we couldn't or didn't see, so it's not!

Carol and I carry parallel Bibles with the English NIV translation on the right hand side of the page and the Spanish Reina Valera 1960 translation on the left hand side of the page. This makes it easier for us to follow the Spanish portions of the services and even helps us improve our Spanish language skills. The RV-1960 is the equivalent of our King James Version, it is THE standard translation used in Mexico. As it turns out, Carol accidentally left her Bible at the church on our last night there. People were milling around everywhere hugging and talking and saying goodbye and in all the hubbub, she left here Bible behind.

As you will read more about in the next chapter, I traveled back to Mexico in February of 2003 with Dr. Cox and some other men of the GBA to further our partnership between the Mexican and Texan Baptist associations and scope out new opportunities for service. We were not scheduled to return to 16 de Septiembre, but since we would be in the neighborhood, I asked if we could just drop in and see if by chance Carol's Bible had been set aside.

My travel mates agreed to the stop over so we made a call and "luckily" found a contact who would meet us at the church for a few minutes. When we arrived we received our surprise. Not just one or two people but nearly the entire congregation of Monte Horeb had turned out to greet us, and with less than four hours notice!

One of the ladies went scurrying off to her house to pick up Carol's Bible. In her excitement that the Texans were coming back she came to the church without the reason for our return visit. One of the deacons of the church, Hermano Goyo, was all smiles as he showed us around and explained what had been happening there since we left.

We'll start with the building project. We had left enough money behind to allow them to finish out their new Sunday School rooms with doors and windows and a floor. They had taken the monies and completed the work.

Not only was the work complete, but as you can see in the pictures, they were putting the rooms to good use.

In Feb 2003 we toured Monte Horeb and find a roof, finished walls, doors, windows, a floor - all the comforts of home!

More exciting than the roof is the evidence of God's word being taught to the children!

This was indeed exciting news, but not near as exciting as what we were to learn next. It seems that while nobody had made a commitment of faith during our

On Mission in Mexico

summer trip, many of the local congregation had experienced true revival in the sense that their spirits had been revived. When we wrapped up our VBS work we had enough left over materials to accommodate another 50 people. We left everything behind, bringing nothing back with us. With their spirits refreshed, the congregation at Monte Horeb had taken these materials up the road a few kilometers to the next ejido and conducted VBS there for the children of that little town.

It really is exciting to see the work being multiplied like this. You just never know how far God will extend His blessing when you go on a trip like one of these!

They spread out in the front yard of a local man named Hermano Angel, and had over 20 kids participate. They used the craft and lesson materials that we had left behind, and answered the call of God to "go ye therefore."

Diez y Seis de Septiembre

In July of 2002 we conducted VBS at Monte Horeb in the town of 16th de Septembre. The folks there took the leftover supplies and conducted VBS at the next little town up the road.

They had taken pictures of their efforts, just like they had seen us do, and were grinning from ear to ear as they gave us copies of these pictures and shared how God had blessed them with our visit and then blessed them again when they went out to share the good news themselves.

Spiritual Lesson #7

God has a plan. He may share it with you. He may not. The work is His. Just go and do what He tells you to do and trust Him to take care of the rest.

I had returned to Texas in July of 2002 thinking our trip was a bust. God had a plan – it just wasn't the plan I was expecting. Good thing He's in charge, isn't it?

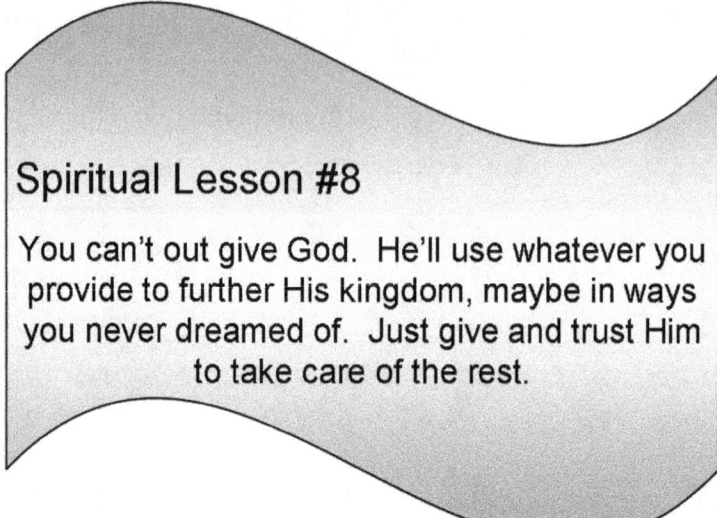

Spiritual Lesson #8

You can't out give God. He'll use whatever you provide to further His kingdom, maybe in ways you never dreamed of. Just give and trust Him to take care of the rest.

We had no idea how God had been working since we had left, but God had a plan and was busily working out that plan as He saw fit. We had no idea what would become of the extra materials, but God had a plan for them before we even left them there.

The name of the ejido where the extra materials were used is Faja de Oro which is Spanish for Belt of Gold. You will read more about Faja de Oro in Chapter 7 as this became the focus of our attention for several years to come.

As for Iglésia Monte Horeb in 16 de Septiembre, Hermano Goyo, his wife Cecilia, and the congregation there have become like family to us. We stop in to visit with them every time we travel to that part of Mexico and have celebrated with them over the years the marriage of their daughters and the births of their grandchildren. In the summer of 2004 we showed the Jesus video there. The mission at Faja de Oro was their mission from the very beginning. We have been their partner to help get things rolling, but we had nothing to do with selecting Faja de Oro as a mission site. God made that selection through Iglésia Monte Horeb and just allowed us to participate, for which we are extremely grateful.

When we were there in the summer of 2006 they expressed a need to obtain a van or bus to help provide transportation for all the children who wanted to come to church. Upon my return to Texas I mentioned this in Sunday School. Not as a "gotta have it or else" but just casually mentioned as an expressed need. The next day I received a telephone call from one of our members saying they had a minivan that they would like to donate.

Diez y Seis de Septiembre

It took us several months to figure out the appropriate paper work to take a van to Mexico and transfer the title to them, but in November of 2007 a small group of us made a trip down there to deliver that minivan.

This picture of the van was taken as we were preparing to hold evening services in the ejido of El Limonál, but that's a whole other story - which you can read about in Chapter 8!

I saw these good friends again in November of 2008 and am happy to report that years later they are still growing, both numerically as well as spiritually, and still excited about being part of God's master plan. I watched incredulously as they piled 15 and 16 people into that minivan to get people to church, and cried with them when we had to part company once more.

Chapter 5: GBA Recon II

The GBA summer mission trip was so successful that planning for the next year began immediately upon our return to Texas. You may recall that the priority list we generated in January of 2002 was almost completely covered during our summer of 2002 trip. We therefore thought it prudent to schedule another recon trip to see where else God was working. Circumstances prevented our GBA Executive Director of Missions from joining us on the 2002 recon trip but wild horses couldn't stop Kyle Cox from leading the way in February of 2003 as six men traveled to Mexico to visit with the President of the Bethsaida Baptist Convention, Hermano Julian De Luna. In addition to Dr. Cox, our recon team included Jack Groebner, pastor of Calvary Baptist Church in Texas City, Jerry Waye, Pastor of Rockview Church in Texas City, Marcelo Garcia, pastor of Primera Iglésia Bautista in Dickinson, Arturo, pastor of another small Hispanic congregation, and me, the token engineer. If you don't think God has a sense of humor, try to imagine one Type-A engineer spending a week in close quarters traveling hundreds of miles with a car full of pastors!

Our initial destination was city of Tampico, home town of Hermano Julian de Luna, President of the Bethsaida Baptist Convention. After checking into the Tampico Inn we made contact and were informed of the plans that had been made regarding our visit. The first change of plans we encountered was that Hermano Julian wanted Kyle and myself to stay at his home and would not take no for an answer. I ended up in his grown daughter's

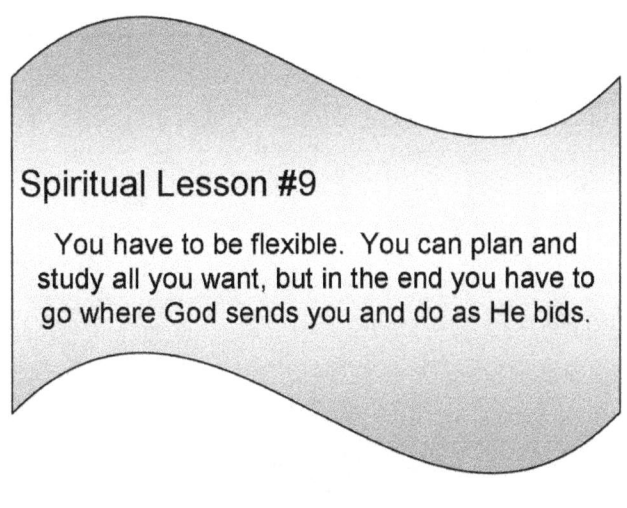

Spiritual Lesson #9

You have to be flexible. You can plan and study all you want, but in the end you have to go where God sends you and do as He bids.

former bedroom, surrounded by dolls and all manner of frilly things! God's sense of humor was working overtime on this trip.

On Mission in Mexico

Mrs. De Luna prepared breakfast and dinner for us each day.. Their children brought their grandchildren to visit with us in the evenings as well. While not part of our original plans, this turned out to be one of the major blessings of the trip!

A couple of us (Dr. Kyle Cox is seated on the left) were blessed to spend a couple of days in the De Luna's home.

Our first serious order of business was to meet with as many of the convention pastors as could make the trip.

We met in one of the local churches with as many pastors as could make it there. Convention President Julian De Luna addresses the group first.

After the large group meeting we traveled around the area for the next several days meeting as many of these folks as we could on their home turf., in the end, coming up with another listing of priority projects where we could see God already at work. That list included:

1. Misión Bautista Betaña in Ciudád Valles
2. Nazarét (Mission of Aposento Alto) outside of Tampico
3. Anahuac (Mission of Aposento Alto) outside of Tampico
4. Vicente Guerrero (Mission of Iglésia Emanuel) outside of Ciudád Mante
5. Santa Júlia (Mission of Principe de Paz) outside of Aldama
6. Carrera Torres (Mission of Principe de Paz) outside of Aldama
7. Getsemaní (Mission of Getsemaní) in Alta Mira (North of Tampico)
8. Movimiento de Fe (Mission of Eliacim) outside of Tampico
9. Puerto Angusto (Mission of Aposento Alto) outside of Tampico
10. Iglésia Bautista Getsemaní (Mission of Primera Iglésia Valles) ouside of Ebano
11. Bautista Betsaida in Ciudád Valles
12. Diez y Seis de Septiembre outside of Ciudád Mante

Another lesson we learned on this trip: ***Where He leads us we will follow: What He feeds us we will swallow.*** One of the local deacons hosted us for dinner one night. As this man was a fisherman, we had fresh seafood. Ever eaten fried egg sack from a pregnant fish? Neither had I until that night.

We were also blessed with some of local delicacies. At this deacon's home we were served a seafood dinner. Jerry Waye, pastor of Rockview church is on the left looking back this way. In the foreground is Jack Groebner, pastor of Calvary Baptist Texas City.

Our mission accomplished, after several days and hundreds of miles of travel, we returned to Texas to see if God was calling any of our local churches to partner with any of these opportunities in Mexico. Some of the churches that had participated the previous year were unable to continue their work in Mexico, others were excited to return. In July 2003 the GBA was to send 4 teams back into Mexico.

Rather than show you pictures of the places we put on the list, since we would only minister to four of the twelve opportunities we'll devote the next chapter to showing you how those teams fared.

Brother Marcelo Garcia, pastor of Primera Iglesia Bautista, Dickinson at the Tampico Inn. He was instrumental in the success of the GBA Mexico Missions efforts and is sorely missed.

Chapter 6: GBA Follow-up Trips 2003

The Galveston Baptist Association was able to form 4 teams to travel into Mexico during the summer of 2003. These teams selected the top 4 priority opportunities from the list we had generated, and off they went. (Carol and I were unable to participate in the July 2003 trips due to a wedding in the family the same weekend.)

Primera Iglésia Bautista Dickinson ministered in Vicente Guerrero once again.

Calvary Baptist Church Texas City ministered in Anahuac, an island just south of Tampico.

Pine Drive Baptist Church Dickinson ministered at Misión Nazarét just outside of Tampico.

Rockview Church ministered at Betaña in Ciudad Valles.

We have already provided you with the "rest of the story" regarding Vicente Guerrero, so you know that as of 2003 they had a building with a roof and four walls but no doors or windows and that they were already packing out the building for services.

Calvary Baptist Texas City enjoyed the balmy weather of the island of Anahuac.

The mission in Anahuac is a mission of Aposento Alto.

Bro. Jack preaches while Dr. Kyle Cox translates at Aposento Alto.

GBA Follow-up Trips

Everybody tries to get under the available shade.

On Mission in Mexico

Maureen (Pastor Jack's wife) keeps 'em working

Craft time

On Mission in Mexico

Pine Drive Dickinson was also close to Tampico at Misión Nazarét.

When they say their mission is just four walls, they're not kidding!

As you can see, their facilities were very rustic!

VBS – Bible Stories, Songs, Games, etc.

GBA Follow-up Trips

The guys had to set up every day.

Add a tarp, an awning, a tree or two,
and the heat is hardly noticeable.

Talk about your overflow!

GBA Follow-up Trips

They ran nearly 100 in VBS every day.

Our fourth team, Rockview, ministered in Betaña outside of Ciudad Valles.

Jerry Waye, his team, and interpreters.

Mission Pastor Luis Angel Fernandez and family

This the Betaña worship center. It isn't quite finished yet but it has a roof and lights.

GBA Follow-up Trips

This is their Sunday School space. They run 60 to 70 children every Sunday.

The beginners class doing crafts.

On Mission in Mexico

Hermano Sabino looks on while some of the girls investigate the contents of their gifts bags.

Pastor Waye is about to be mobbed during game time. These guys play rough!

There were dozens of people who made professions of faith during this week long project in the four different missions. God truly blessed.

Chapter 7: Faja de Oro

The beginning of this story you already know. Carol and I were part of the mission team that worked in 16 de Septiembre in July 2002. In July of 2003 Iglésia Monte Horeb was so low on the priority list that there was not a team from the GBA sent to that location, although we did stop in to visit with them one evening since we were working less than 30 minutes away in Vicente Guerrero. As you recall from previous chapters, the folks at Iglésia Monte Horeb took the leftover materials from our visit in 2002 and conducted VBS in the neighboring ejido of Faja de Oro. In 2003, since they didn't have the support of one of the GBA mission teams, they conducted VBS and revival services again on their own. During our brief visit with them in 2003 they mentioned that they felt led to begin a mission at Faja de Oro and asked if we would like to help. Upon our return to Texas Carol and I asked our home church, Arcadia First Baptist in Santa Fe, if they would like to participate in such an activity. The response was positive so we began making plans for the summer of 2004.

The AFBC Mexico 2004 Mission Team

Jim, Jose, Bill, Joe, Carol, Kay, Pam, Betty, Dena, Bettie, Gerald
Katy, Amanda, Jose Luis, Yaritza, Claudia (and Iris)

Along with a family from Primera Iglésia Bautista Dickinson (José and Claudia Rodriquez) we set out for Ciudad Mante in July of 2004.

On Mission in Mexico

Our first full day on the mission field was back at Vicente Guerrero assisting Primera Iglésia Bautista Dickinson with the medical mission there.

Medical Mission - Over 100 served
Two local doctors and one dentist, in addition to our own nurse and EMT

Before you see a doctor, you hear the good news of Jesus Christ from Brother Arturo. Several accepted Christ as Savior on this, our first day on the mission field.

Arrangements had been made in advance with a couple of local Christian doctors to provide medical services for free on the mission site. In addition, our Texas team included a nurse and an EMT who helped with the screening. The staff was rounded out by a Mexican dentist from Monterrey who just happened to be related to José and Claudia.

On Sunday we attended services at Iglésia Monte Horeb and enjoyed a relaxing lunch with them.

Our host church fed us lunch in their fellowship hall . . .

We used this time to discuss the plans they had made to conduct VBS in Faja de Oro and to show them the materials that we had brought with us. Every pencil, crayon, and piece of paper needed to support the VBS craft time was brought with us. We had already learned that the guards at the border will search boxes without a moment's hesitation but rarely opened up suitcases so we had packed enough VBS materials for 150 participants into roughly 50 suitcases that had been donated by H.I.S. Ministries in Santa Fe. This multi-denominational ministry runs (among other things) a resale shop which helps supply funds to some of its other outreach programs. The director of the resale shop (Ruth Crosby) does an outstanding job of using that ministry to minister to other ministries as well as to individuals. When she found out about the need she started setting suitcases aside for us in advance of our trip.

On Mission in Mexico

That same afternoon we traveled out to Faja de Oro so our team could scope out the territory and began planning how we would organize VBS which was slated to start at 9:00 AM on Monday morning.

**This is Brother Angel, his wife Norma, and two of their kids.
They hosted the VBS at their house and in their yard.**

Unlike the mission at Vicente Guerrero, here we did not have access to a vacant lot. Instead God provided us with a family willing to share their corner lot with us. We spread out the best we could with what we had.

**VBS class for the 6 and under crowd
They ran about a dozen every day.**

The 7 and 8 year olds met under the blue tarps and also ran about a dozen every day.

The 9 – 12 year old class met under the green canopies and ran around 20 per day.

The youth and adults met where ever they could find shade.
They ran from 30 to 45 per day.

The big tent was saved for the craft area.
Each class came to this spot for their craft time.

In our very first VBS attempt in this ejido we were running 75 to 100 people in attendance, and all of them coming on foot! Let's see you find 100 people who would walk to VBS in 100+ degree heat in Texas!

Having been in touch with the host church the previous summer and several times during the year between trips, we were aware that a piece of property in this ejido was available for sale at what would be a ridiculously low price by American standards – less than $2,000 for approximately an acre of land. The membership of Arcadia FBC had easily raised the funds to purchase the land for a new church in Faja de Oro while we were there.

The guys show you the paper work for the land purchased with AFBC funds. Below the team stands on that land and gives thanks.

Faja de Oro lies just off the paved highway between Ciudad Mante and Tampico, but there isn't a paved road in the entire village. Approximately 700 people live there. The major crop of the area is sugar cane and many of the inhabitants are employed by the large companies that grow commercial quantities of this grassy plant. This village lies approximately 30 minutes outside of the nearest city and had no churches of any kind located there. The property that we purchased for a new mission there included several rows of sugar cane from the edge of a much larger field. We snacked good that week.

On Mission in Mexico

The 57 meter by 57 meter property includes several rows of sugar cane. (Ours was confiscated at the border.)

In addition to VBS during the day, we traveled around to several churches showing religious films with a projector in the evenings.

We showed the Jesus video to 30 people at Iglésia Monte Horeb in 16th de Septiembre, the Left Behind movie to 90 people at Misión Bautista Peniel at Vicente Guerrero, and the video Apocolyse to 35 people at Iglésia Emmanuel in Ciudad Mante.

We also left another $400 or so behind so the mission at Faja de Oro could install an electrical service pole, file the title paper work and so forth. Arcadia

FBC had agreed to providing support to this mission effort for several years, not just for one summer, so we spent time at the end of the week taking notes regarding what else was needed.

As usual, by the time our week was completed, it was hard to say goodbye.

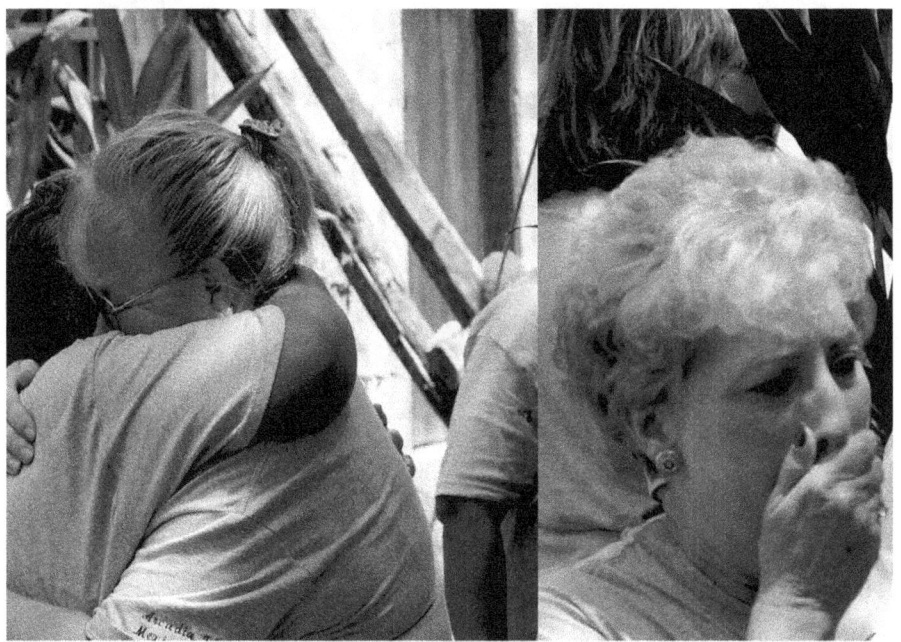

Saying goodbye wasn't easy. We were touched by these kind folks.

The Rest of the Story

The nice part of saying goodbye to Christian friends is knowing that will see them again. Maybe on this side of Heaven or maybe on the other side, but we will all be reunited again some day. When we meet again on the other side of Jordan we won't be so hampered by the language barrier.

While we were gone on the July 2004 trip our own church was conducting VBS back home. The children there collected pennies for Mexico. I think some of them might have cheated and brought more than just pennies because they raised approximately $1,000 to support the mission at Faja de Oro. Combined with other donations this would be more than sufficient to build a fence around the newly purchased property, which is the first step in taking possession of the property.

On Mission in Mexico

The Arcadia FBC collected pennies for Mexico during their 2004 Vacation Bible School. They raised approximately $1,000 which was enough to build the fence at Faja de Oro.

So excited were we about how the mission was developing, several of the men of Arcadia headed back to Mexico in February of 2005 to build fence.

Hermano Benito explains how the process works to us.

Faja de Oro

Then we go to work!

Even the corner posts are built out of concrete!

On Mission in Mexico

Come July of 2005 we were ready to load up the trailer and do it again.

This time we had two families from Primera Iglésia Bautista helping out as Benito and Rosa Aguilera joined the team.

Faja de Oro

Once again we scheduled a medical mission as our first day of ministry. The difference is that this time the medical mission took place in make shift tents and lean-tos on the newly fenced property in Faja de Oro.

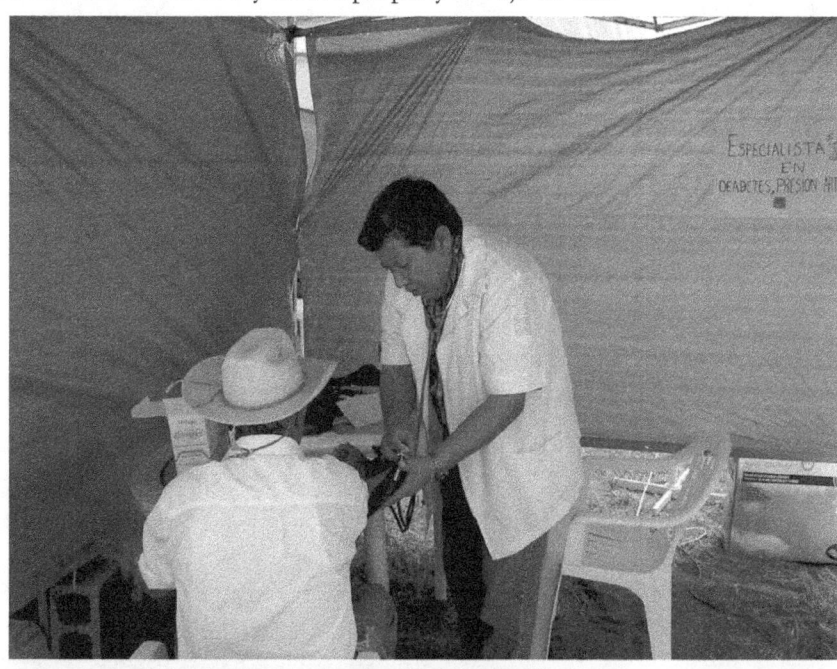

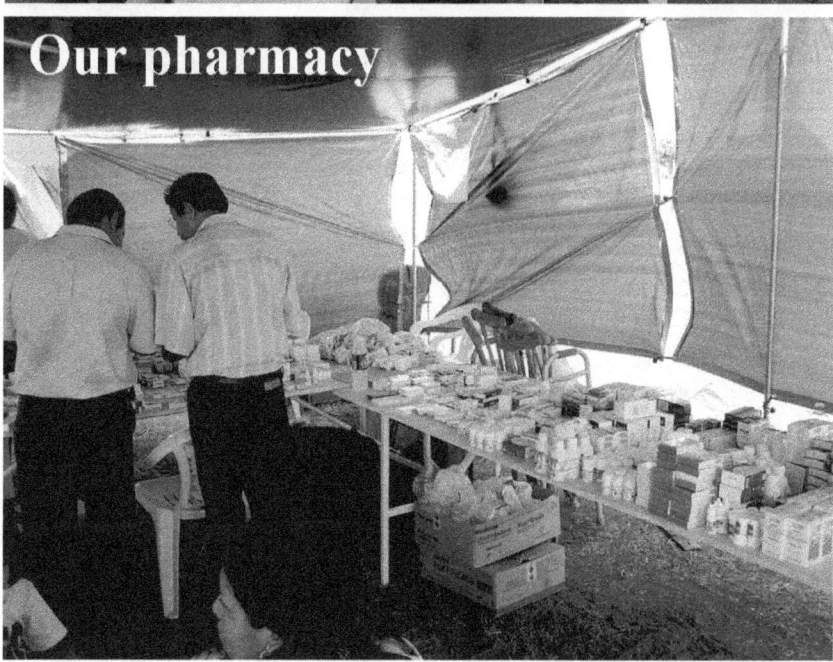

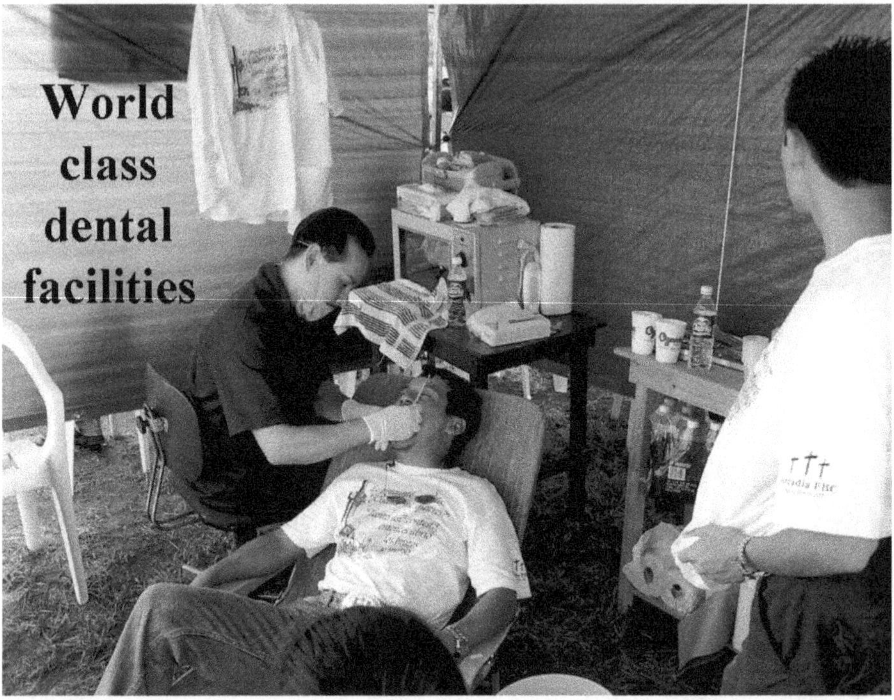

On Mission in Mexico

World class dental facilities

Dr. Jorge, our friendly visiting dentist, made his second appearance to work with us. Until you've had your teeth cleaned sitting in a lawn chair on a dirt floor under a tarp in the tropical heat of the Mexican interior, you just haven't lived.

While the medically trained folks worked on ministering to the physical needs of the locals, the rest of us busied ourselves helping out with the kids, singing, cleaning up, or running errands as need. There was never a shortage of things to do.

One of the chores that we had asked the locals to attend to between our February and July trips was the installation of facilities on the property. This part is going to sound a little odd, but as the saying goes, "The brutal truth is still the truth." By this time I had traveled fairly extensively throughout the southern part of the Mexican state of Tamaulipas and had been graciously received by many people in some pretty rugged outlying areas. One of the things I had come to learn was that my six foot frame was larger than is typical in that part of the world. The mechanism by which I came to learn this great truth was my inability to stand up in a typical Mexican outhouse. (I told you this part was weird.) Before we left in February I visited a workshop where such things were manufactured and placed a special order to have a couple built Texas size. Some things you just can't scrimp on!

And with all the comforts of home . . .

The balance of the week was spent conducting Vacation Bible School classes during the earlier morning hours and returning to Faja de Oro each evening for revival services. Again we saw the Lord move. During that week eight more souls came to a saving knowledge of Jesus Christ and several more asked the minister to come talk with them some more about Jesus.

On Mission in Mexico

This was the second year that my youngest daughter Amanda (below on the right) and her friend Katy (below on the left) accompanied us to the mission field.

Two teenaged girls gave up their chance to attend summer camp with the youth, choosing to serve on the mission field instead. Now THAT'S cool!

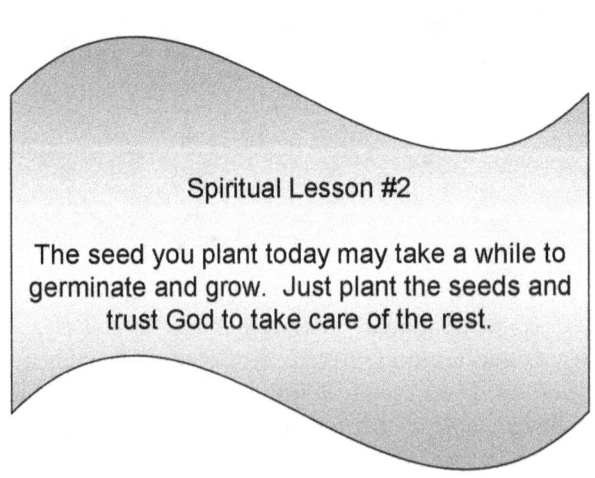

Spiritual Lesson #2

The seed you plant today may take a while to germinate and grow. Just plant the seeds and trust God to take care of the rest.

Both of these girls learned to play the guitar in this general time frame and are now using their abilities to minister elsewhere; Amanda at the University of Mary Hardin-Baylor and Katy on the mission field in Ukraine. Isn't it neat how God takes the smallest little action and sometimes let you see the ripple

Faja de Oro

effect as your action touches somebody else who touches somebody else and so on?

Jose and Claudia Rodriquez

Regina Davis (Center) poses with her local helpers.

On Mission in Mexico

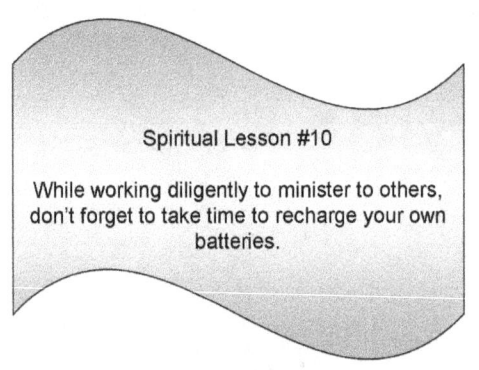

Spiritual Lesson #10

While working diligently to minister to others, don't forget to take time to recharge your own batteries.

One last lesson from this trip, and then we'll continue on with the story. This trip marked the first time that we scheduled some time off for the team. In hind sight we should have always done this, but there was always so much work to do that we just worked every spare minute. On this trip the team took off one afternoon to visit El Nacimiento, which means the birthplace. It is a cave from which comes the water which feeds the lake which feeds the rivers which water the area around Ciudad Mante. Unfortunately, Billy Moore and I had to miss it as we were dealing with a van insurance problem that afternoon.

One of the things we learned was to take an afternoon off to recharge our own batteries. This is a lake called El Nacimiento.

Since we had left in February they had completed the fencing, installed the outdoor facilities, installed the electrical drop, planted grass and trees, and purchased some plastic chairs. The folks at Arcadia had been so generous in their support that we were able to leave funds behind that would pour the foundation footer and floor, build the support columns, walls, and put a roof on the building! Wow! The new mission was named Monte de los Olivos which means Mount of Olives.

Faja de Oro

Again the children at Arcadia First Baptist Church in Santa Fe collected pennies for Mexico, and again the adults gave generously. In July 2006 we returned to Faja de Oro to find Misión Monte de los Olivos coming along nicely.

They now have a church building!

The building, or temple as they would call it, is dried in but still in pretty rough shape. Still, it marks a special time for them as we are able this week to get in out of the weather for services. The rough nature of the building didn't seem to bother anybody, they were all just happy for what the Lord had provided.

On Mission in Mexico

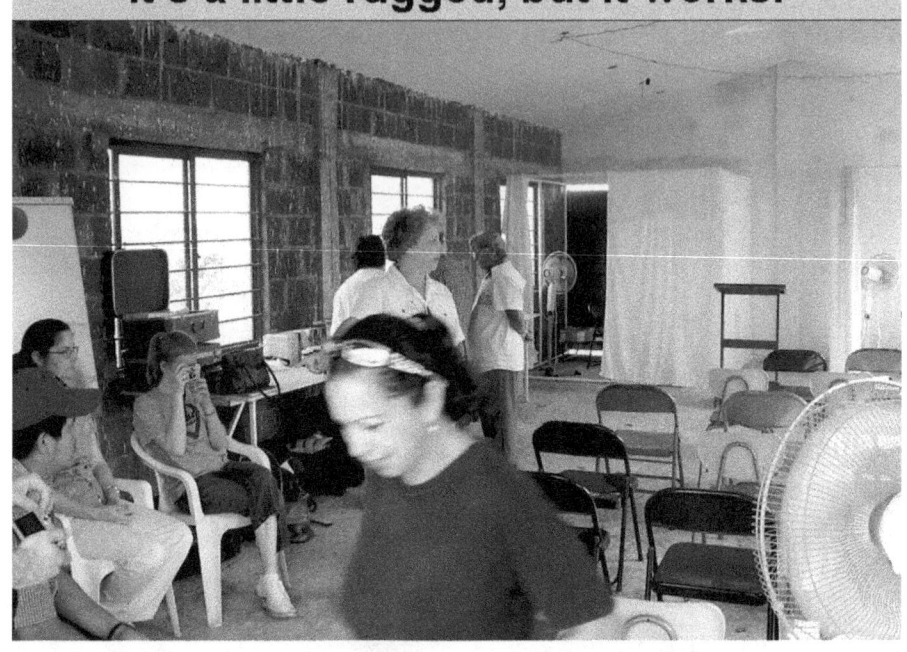
It's a little rugged, but it works.

Regina and Amanda seem to be happy to be back . . .

Faja de Oro

Billy Moore looks like he's having a good time as well.

We have hundreds of photos and video clips of our trip, but what you would see is more of the same. The adults and youth met inside the new building and the remainder of the VBS classes met outside under tarps and tents again.

Several more people come to know Jesus as Savior, and the mission continues to grow both numerically as well as spiritually.

In July 2007 AFBC musters a small team to return for what we expect to be the last ministerial visit to Faja de Oro since the mission is so strong. Being unable to accompany them on this trip due to our oldest daughter's wedding I have no pictures to share from July, but I was able to make a quick trip to Mexico in November of 2007 and can show you the mission at that point. (The November 2007 trip was to deliver the donated van that I talked about in the previous chapter.)

In November of 2007 we find the mission basically finished, inside and out. They are meeting there weekly, have a strong congregation, and are excited to have a church in their town where they can worship the Lord together.

November of 2007: A coat of paint on the outside . . .

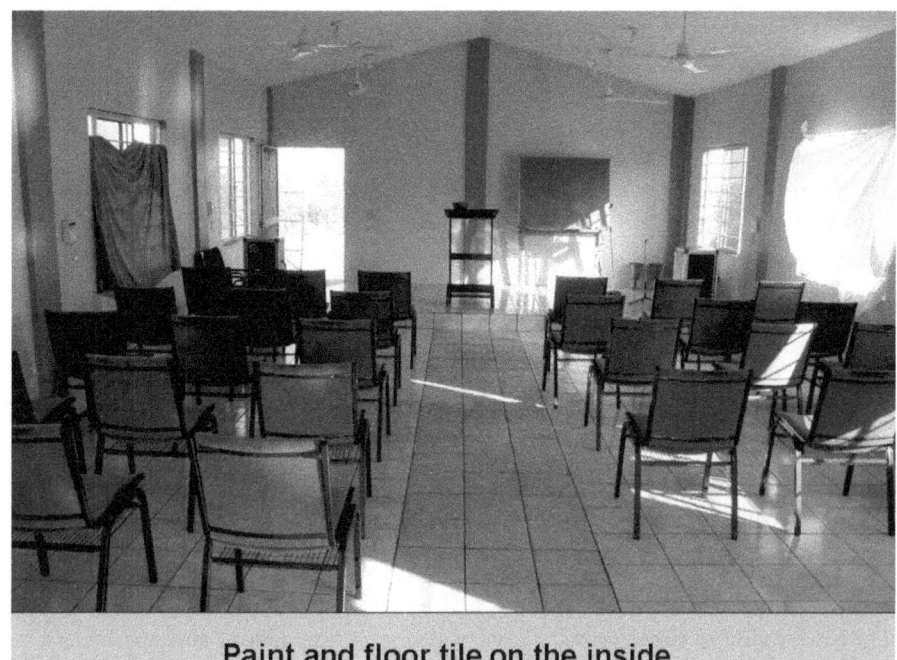

Paint and floor tile on the inside.

Services now take place indoors in a pretty little church building.

In fact they had grown so strong that they were working on a mission opportunity of their own, in the ejido of El Limonál, located approximately two hours away in the state of San Luis Potosi.

We were excited to find out that they were doing exactly what the Lord commanded when he told us all to "go ye therefore" and spread the good news. One of the things it means to me personally is that this then is not the end of the story, just the end of one chapter and the beginning of yet another!

> **Spiritual Lesson #11**
>
> A little bit goes a long way in the hands of the Lord. Don't hold back because you don't think you have enough. Just give and trust God to multiply your offering.

The total cost to buy the land, fence it, and build a pretty little church building on the property was approximately $13,000 spread out over 4 years. While this sounds like a lot of money, and it is to any one person, when you consider that many churches in the U.S. spend that much on their sound and video projection systems, this is really a drop in the bucket. A little bit goes a long way in Mexico.

Chapter 8: El Limonál

This chapter will be pretty short, because the story has only just begun. The layman from Iglésia Monte Horeb in 16 de Septiembre who was largely responsible for the mission work at Faja de Oro was Hermano Goyo. His wife Cecilia was born and raised in the neighboring state of San Luis Potosi in a little ejido called El Limonál. Somewhere in the 2006 timeframe, while Misión Monte de los Olivos in Faja de Oro was being built, these folks made a visit back to the old homestead. While there, they did what all good Christians do, they talked about Jesus. One thing led to another, and they were asked to help start a mission in El Limonál because they too had no Christian influence of any denomination in their village.

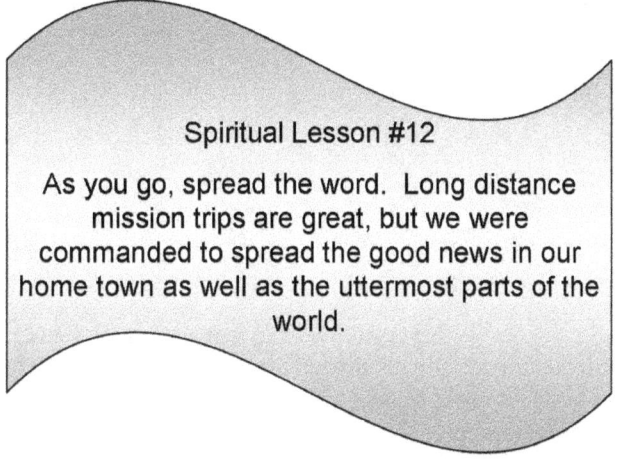

Spiritual Lesson #12

As you go, spread the word. Long distance mission trips are great, but we were commanded to spread the good news in our home town as well as the uttermost parts of the world.

The minivan that was donated to the mission efforts at 16 de Septiembre and Faja de Oro was also being used to transport workers to El Limonál for services on Saturdays. To get to El Limonál you have to drive approximately 2 hours from 16 de Septiembre across several very rugged mountains and through a couple of the most beautiful scenic valleys you can imagine. During our trip to deliver the minivan in 2007 we were blessed to participate in special services being held in the front yard of one of the locals.

With only a few days notice of our coming, over 30 people turned out for services that ran well past sunset. This ejido is higher up in the mountains and when the sun goes down, so does the thermometer. The temperature dropped into the 60's that evening and it was interesting to see the locals pulling out their heaviest winter coats.

On Mission in Mexico

El Limonál – in the front yard of Hermano Andres

As we had seen in our other work in Mexico, they made due with whatever space they could find.

Children's Church was on the front porch.

El Limonál

By the time we returned in November of 2008 to visit with our contacts there, we find all is well at Iglésia Monte Horeb in 16 de Septiembre and at Misión Monte de los Olivos in Faja de Oro. The mission at Faja de Oro is so strong that they are working hard on establishing a full fledged mission at El Limonál.

An unoccupied piece of river front property has been identified as available for sale for $12,000 USD. The property includes a two room house a couple of other smaller structures. The owner, currently living outside of Dallas, Texas is willing to hold it for them in order to help get the mission established.

The main building on the property at El Limonál.

He's also willing to work out any kind of deal that he can to help them get into the property permanently. In the meantime, he offered the mission free use of the grounds anytime they need it for gatherings.

Once again we look at the numbers and think $12,000 is a lot of money but a drop in the bucket compared to the cost of repainting the parking lots of most of our churches or remodeling our fellowship halls.

Unfinished building on the property. We used it for children's church.

The total cost of this property with three existing buildings is roughly equivalent to the cost of buying property and building Misión Monte de los Olivos in Faja de Oro.

The 3rd building is not much more than a storage shack.

El Limonál

We were only able to stay for a couple of days in November of 2008, but we were blessed to see a strong mission group already meeting here.

In November 2008 we had 35 adults and 15 children for revival services.

Children's church is in a little side building.

On Mission in Mexico

The adults gathered outside under some huge (50 foot tall) fichus trees while the children were able to use one of the smaller out buildings. Hermano Benito sang and preached, and several of the locals came forward to give testimonies. There is something very special about these outdoor gatherings that I just can't seem to find words for. People willing to sit outside in the weather to go to church REALLY want to be in church.

Hermano Benito leads the singing.

We don't know yet what God has in store for El Limonál or if we are supposed to be a part of it. We believe that this part of the story is just beginning and we look forward to seeing what God is up to.

One last story to add to the spiritual truth that God can take a seemingly insignificant act of obedience and multiply it ways you cannot dream of. This is a picture of Sulema, a teenaged girl from Faja de Oro, playing the guitar and singing at the new mission in El Limonál. She learned how to play on a guitar donated by somebody at Arcadia FBC in 2005 or 2006. Today she's helping to minister to others. God is good – all the time!

Chapter 9: "Typical" mission trip itineraries

The title of this chapter is a little misleading. We've been on many mission trips over a period of many years I don't think anything is ever typical, but since people often ask me what a typical trip looks like, here goes nothing.

When working with new congregations in outlying rural areas, there are two main types of services we try to provide: Vacation Bible School and Revival Services. If the town with the hotel is close enough, we try to conduct VBS from 9:00 AM to Noon, take a few hours off in the middle of the afternoon to rest up (siesta time) then come back in the evening hours for services. Many businesses in Mexico are often closed for a couple of hours in middle of the afternoon, so this isn't the best time to visit the market place, but sometimes it is the only free time we have. As we've mentioned before, many times our teams use the afternoons to clean up, cool off, and prepare for the evening services and/or for VBS the next day.

We try to break down the VBS attendees by age group so that the folks attending can learn at a relatively similar pace. If we have enough help we will offer a class for babies through preschool so the kids who can't read can all play together. Having a nursery allows some adult woman to attend who might not otherwise get the opportunity. The younger learners may include the 6-8 year olds. The middle class is the 9 to 12 folks and then we offer a youth/adult class. In the U.S. you will not typically see adults participating in VBS but this is very common in Mexico. In order to have 4 classes you have to have at least 4 teachers who are fluent in Spanish and it would be better to have a helper for each class, although the helper doesn't have to be bi-lingual. To take some of the load off of the teachers we have a separate craft staff that prepares and executes the craft portion of VBS. This might be 1, 2 or 3 people but at least one of them has to be able to give instructions in Spanish. We have been blessed to have some teenagers accompany us on mission trips and we usually leave recreation time up to them. Lastly we have a person or two in charge of making sure we have enough cookies, napkins, kool-aid, cups, etc. on hand for refreshment time. If you can get enough help, it is always handy to have one person left over to be the gopher or runner. With a staff of anywhere from 7 to 15 people and over 100 participants, there is always something that needs doing outside of the stuff you planned for!

Because of the children's school schedules, they are only off for about 4 weeks in July, we typically conduct VBS beginning on the weekend around the 4th of July. This ensures that the target audience is available to participate, and allows many of our team to make the trip with less vacation time because the trip occurs over a traditional U.S. Holiday. Just a thought.

On Mission in Mexico

It takes several folks who are bilingual to support an Anglo team in Mexico. Conversational Spanish is one thing – fluency that is sufficient to teach a VBS class is a whole other matter. When you run short of translators, you would be amazed at how effective people become at sign language and pantomime. To overcome the issue of translation, we have found it best to partner with an Hispanic congregation. Together we can do great things.

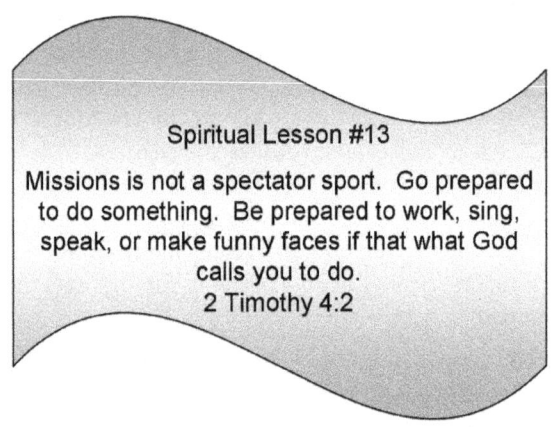

Spiritual Lesson #13

Missions is not a spectator sport. Go prepared to do something. Be prepared to work, sing, speak, or make funny faces if that what God calls you to do.
2 Timothy 4:2

The evening services are very traditional. They will have a time of singing and worship in song, then a time of preaching. Be prepared to participate. Often times there is a time of testimony that we have seen last nearly an hour as over half of the congregation had something they wanted to share. We have also seen folks come down front and ask for prayer then a 30 minute prayer meeting break out. The bottom line is you need to be flexible to let the Holy Spirit drive the service. A two hour evening service is perfectly normal, and it may not start until 30 or 45 minutes late. It is VERY common to have twice as many people there at the end of the service as were there when the service started. Punctuality is one of the topics we'll cover in the Chapter 11 on the culture.

Several communities that we visited as part of our Galveston Baptist Association planning trips specifically asked us to provide prayer teams. They wanted people who would come to revival services that they would hold and just pray the entire time. They also asked for teams to conduct prayer walks. "Just come to our village and walk the streets with us praying for the souls that are here." They didn't ask for money, or VBS materials, or singers, or preachers - just somebody who would commit to coming and praying with them. Here's a task that any Christian should be able to fulfill.

Somewhat harder to do, but still worth the effort, is showing religious films at various churches. The films themselves are easily available both in the states and in Mexico, but hauling the equipment around is a little of a challenge. We took an LCD projector and carried a combo VHS/DVD player with us. We also carried a little Fender PA system with us with a couple of portable speakers and a nice long extension cord. When you can do this you are almost guaranteed a good turn out as a free movie is quite a draw. The local preachers love it when you can draw a big crowd, because then they can share the gospel

Typical Itineraries

and offer an invitation. The drawbacks to this are the heat and the utilities. More than once I wondered if my projector would survive being run in the 100+ degree heat for several hours. Most electrical outlets in Mexico are two pronged and ungrounded. You will need a long extension cord and an adapter or be willing to cut off the ground lug and then leave the cord there – as we did the first time we attempted to use our equipment south of the border.

Some of the mission teams that we have discussed so far have attempted both VBS and evening services. On some of our shorter (less than 4 day) trips all we attempted was evening services. Other teams accepted work assignments so far away from their accommodations that they were not physically able to come and go twice in one day, so they either conducted VBS or evening services, but not both. What you do on your trip will depend on where you are working and where you are staying and what the folks down there ask for and how God directs you. Our only advice is to think through your daily activities and make sure you have at least a chance of getting it all done.

Other activities that we have accomplished on various mission trips:

1. On one trip the ladies of the mission team held an evening gathering for the local ladies. I wasn't invited but I understand they had a women's Bible study, a foot washing, and gave pedicures.

2. We almost always take along as many suitcases of donated clothes as we can carry. We set up tables one afternoon between VBS and the evening services and make the clothes available to the locals, many of whom struggle to obtain nice things.

3. We almost always take along 100 to 200 zip lock baggies of goodies for the VBS participants. Each baggie will have pencils, pens, erasers, sharpeners, a comb, a wash rag, a bar of soap, a little bottle of shampoo, a tooth brush, a little tube of toothpaste, some hard candy, and a small toy or two. These gift bags are unbelievably popular with kids and adults alike. (When you consider the VBS craft materials, the clothes, the gift bags, and the luggage for the team, you can see why we pull a trailer ...)

4. On nearly all of our mission trips we have been approached by somebody who had a sick relative or a sick friend that they wanted us to visit and pray for. More than once we have driven over an hour away to spend 15 minutes praying for somebody who was really too sick to host company. If the logistics work out we may take the entire team on this trip. Sometimes we just send a couple of representatives because the rest of the team is busy with other scheduled work.

5. We discussed medical missions in a couple of the earlier chapters. This is a fantastic way to draw a crowd, but much more difficult to schedule.

In our trips the medical expertise was provide by local doctors, dentists, and pharmacists who are Christian and sympathetic to the cause. Arranging this in advance and supplying money to purchase medicines in advance assumes you have made contacts with the right people on previous trips and have the ability to plans months ahead of your trip. You may not pull one of these off on the first trip, but maybe you could on your second trip south.

6. You saw in Chapter 7 that we conducted a construction trip at Faja de Oro to help them build fence. We brought the funds, purchased the materials, and then worked side by side with our new brothers in Christ to erect the fence. Spending time like this working together is an excellent way to practice your Spanish and get to know your co-workers. I highly recommend conducting this type of activity in the winter months when the day time temperatures cool off to the 60's and 70's. Doing this kind of physical labor in July would have killed me.

Regardless of what God calls you to do, if you do it out of obedience and with a glad heart, He will bless your efforts. You may see the blessing while you're there or you may not know about what mighty things He has done for many years to come – if ever – but He will bless your efforts.

One final note on what to do on your mission trip: Take an afternoon or a day off to see the local sights and have a little fun. We haven't always done this, and in hind sight we haven't always done it right. It is important to keep your team energized and not work them completely into the ground. It is also a excellent opportunity to share this "down time" with your local workers and get to know them better while building a working relationship with

them. Close to Ciudad Mante is the cave where the water that forms the lake which feeds the local rivers comes from. They call it "El Nacimiento" which means the birth place. In the mountains around El Limonál there are many cascadas, or waterfalls that absolutely stunningly beautiful. I'm not in favor of mission trips that are 4 day vacations with a ½ day ministry effort tacked on, but taking a little time off to let your team rest and see the sights is a very good thing to do.

Carol, Rosa & Linda at La Cascada Meca

Benito and the ladies by the river.

El Mercado in Ciudad Mante.

Chapter 10: Working in Mexico

(A collection of tips we've learned, often the hard way)

Passports & Travel Visas

Getting into Mexico is not too difficult, especially if you are just barely going across the border. The region within about 20 miles of the border is called La Frontera – The Frontier – and is easily accessible by foot or by automobile without any kind of travel visa or permit. To get back into the United States requires a valid U.S. Passport these days. Because of this relatively recent ruling we require all members of the mission team to have and carry a valid U.S. Passport no matter how far into Mexico we are traveling. Here is a link to the government website where you can download the application form and start the ball rolling:

http://travel.state.gov/passport/passport_1738.html

The forms are different for adults and minors, and the form for a renewal is different than the form for a first time applicant, so make sure you download the correct form for your needs. An adult applying for the first time would use form DS-11. Take a completed but unsigned DS-11 along with two passport photos and acceptable proof of citizenship (birth certificate) to a local passport agency. You must apply in person and you must sign the DS-11 in the presence of the passport official. The passport photos can be obtained for less than $10 from places like Walgreens or CVS Pharmacy. The website above will provide complete instructions and even help you locate the nearest Acceptance Facility, which is often located in a Post Office facility. At the time of this writing, the Acceptance Office charged $55 for the passport and $30 as an application fee. Add another $10 or so for the passport photos and you are looking at nearly $100 to obtain your new passport. If you don't have a copy of your birth certificate you can contact the county clerk's office in the county where you were born and obtain one – for a fee of course.

The processing time for your passport varies depending on the time of the year and what's going on in the world, but you will need to allow at least 4 weeks so don't wait until the week before you are supposed to leave to take care of this. Start early and avoid headaches later.

To travel deeper into Mexico than the border towns of the frontier requires a travel visa. If you are staying for 7 days or less this is a free document that you apply for and receive at the border. All you have to do is fill out a little form that provides them with some personal information, such as your Passport number, and tells them where you plan to go, where you will be staying, and for how long. Be prepared to stand in line. We have taken fairly large groups into Mexico several times. Sometimes they will pass out the visa applications and let everybody fill them out simultaneously. Sometimes they ask you to sit at a desk in front of them and fill them out one at a time.

If your trip will last longer than 7 days, you will need a slightly different visa. The application form is the same but you have to pay a fee of $11 to obtain permission to stay more than a week. This fee will validate your travel visa for 6 months. Each person should keep this visa with them at all times. When asked for your papers by the authorities (and they will ask) you need to be able to produce evidence that you have permission to be where you are.

Vehicle Permits

Just like with personal visas, you can travel into the frontier border areas without a special vehicle permit, but to travel any deeper into the interior than that requires one. We have had more trouble with vehicle permits over the years than anything else. Either the rules change annually, or the local border guards are very inconsistent about what is and what is not required – or maybe both. Our July 2002 mission trip included a lot of people from a lot of churches and 11 vehicles. We arrived at the border around 5PM to begin processing all of our permits. At 2:00AM the next morning we gave up on one of them and made the decision to leave a truck in the parking lot of a church in Harlingen. With that introduction here's what seems to work the best:

- The best and only fool proof option is that you have clear title – the original not a photocopy – to the vehicle and it must be in the name of the person crossing the border.

- If the vehicle is in more than one name (e.g. husband and wife) then either both parties have to be present at the border crossing or the party staying behind has to provide written authorization to take the vehicle to Mexico. This is supposedly to prevent one half of the married couple from stealing the family car from the other half and disappearing across the border.

- If the title is not clear then you must have written permission from the lien holder to take the vehicle to Mexico. Make sure this written permission includes the description of the vehicle, the Vehicle Identification Number, and the dates that the vehicle is expected to be in Mexico. The permission letter has to specifically name the party responsible for the vehicle. A generic "the mission team is given permission" letter does not work.

- If the vehicle is borrowed or rented, you need written permission granting you authorization to take the vehicle into Mexico, again with

Working in Mexico

description, VIN, and dates of travel. Only a few rental car companies will allow their vehicles to travel to Mexico, so check on this well in advance. Capps Van Rental in Texas allows this and will provide the necessary written permission letter in both English and Spanish.

- One way that we managed to take a borrowed van across in 1993 was to have the owner transfer ownership of the van to me a couple of months prior to making the trip. Upon our return I transferred ownership back to the real owner. It made it easy at the border to represent myself as the sole owner of the vehicle.

- If you have an accident in Mexico and don't have Mexican insurance, you can expect to go to jail – go directly to jail – without passing go! In Mexico you are NOT innocent until proven guilty. They have a completely different justice system and you DON'T want to experience it first hand. Their system is that you get locked up while the liabilities are being sorted out. You can avoid this by carrying Mexican car insurance, which can be purchased for days or weeks at a time. We have tried several different companies over the years and in our experience Sanborns Insurance is the cheapest, most reliable, and easiest to obtain. They have offices all along the border and do business over the internet as well. In recent years Capps Van Rental has become a licensed agent of Sanborns so that you can rent the van and obtain the permission and insurance documents all at the same time. Very convenient.

- Trailers are not really vehicles, but depending on the whim of the border guards they may require you to purchase a vehicle permit for a towed trailer as well. Better to go prepared with clear title, permission letters, etc., and not need these things than to show up at the border and not be allowed to take your luggage and supplies across.

- There is an entire section of this chapter devoted to your luggage and supplies and the issues we've had getting materials across the border.

The vehicle permit costs around $60 in U.S. dollars and can ONLY be paid for with a credit card. They will not accept cash. One person told us this is because they will bill your credit card for the value of the vehicle if you don't bring it back within the specified guidelines. Another border guard said he didn't think that was true.

Once you have all of your permits and visas in place – and this may take a few hours – you can drive through the border checkpoint. The border guards may waive you through or they may pull you over for inspection. If you don't have all the necessary paperwork, be prepared for a long delay. After getting through this spot you can head into the interior. More than once we have been pulled over by the local police in the next town and had them question the validity of our paperwork. Usually they are looking for an offer to pay a small fine – on the spot – to remedy the situation and let you go on your way. Having somebody on the trip that understands the culture and can handle these issues is absolutely critical. Speaking Spanish is one thing. Understanding Spanish is a whole other story. We strongly recommend partnering with people that are part of the Mexican culture. We have even had folks from hundreds of miles south of the border take a bus, meet us at the border, and escort us to our destination. This isn't always necessary, but it underscores the importance in understanding the differences between our cultures. At about the 20 or 25 mile mark you will come to a frontier checkpoint. You will be expected to show your personal and vehicular permits and may be asked to exit the vehicle while it is searched. This is just part of the adventure: better that you should be prepared for it than surprised by it. We have also been detained and searched on the road home at various federal check points. We have never been mistreated, threatened, harassed, or harmed in any way, nor have we ever lost anything in these searches. It is just part of the game.

Driving in Mexico

A special driver's license is not required in Mexico, but Carol and I both carry International Drivers Permits. This link to the U.S. State Department website will tell you a little more about these:

http://travel.state.gov/travel/tips/safety/safety_1179.html

An IDP not difficult to obtain and, as you will see on the State Dept. website, can be applied for at AAA offices throughout the United States for about $15. Just like with the title for your trailer, in our opinion it is better to have more documentation that you think you need than to get in trouble and not have the right stuff. Here's the link to their website if you are interested:

http://www.aaa.com/vacation/idpf.html

With or without an International Drivers Permit, driving in Mexico is not for the faint of heart! The roads are narrow and poorly maintained. Speed limits are apparently more of a suggestion than a law. Right of way is often a matter of who has the most guts. In many cases it appears that the traffic laws are not enforced routinely, but only exist to determine who is at fault in case of an accident. A major highway may in fact only be one lane in each direction, with a shoulder almost as wide as a driving lane – but not quite. People will pull to the right hand shoulder to allow you to more easily pass. They may even turn on their left turn signal as a message to you that it is safe to come around their left side. Mexican drivers almost never use their turn signals to indicate that they are turning.

Working in Mexico

The Mexican Tourism Ministry operates a fleet of several hundred pickup trucks known as the Angeles Verdes, or Green Angels, which is similar to the AAA in the United States. If you break down on the road these folks are cruising around with all the tools needed to jump start your car, change a flat tire, provide a couple of gallons of gas, etc. The services are free except for cost of parts, but tipping is very much appreciated. We have only seen one of these trucks on the road during all our many miles of travel in Mexico, and 300 trucks is not many when it comes to covering the whole country, so you may not want to rely on them being there when you need them. If you need help on the road you can call 060 which is the Mexican equivalent of 911 in the states.

A road side service that we have needed more than once is that of a Vulcanizadora – which is a tire repair shop. Don't expect these to look fancy, but they can repair a flat in no time and have you on the move again. Once, in 2001 we had a piece of rebar cut a gash in the side wall of the tire of my Chevy van. In the U.S. this type of destruction is not repairable. The Mexican tire shop fixed that tire and it is still on the van and still being used in 2008. How often you need the services of a vulcanizadora depends on where you travel and under what conditions. Our record was 7 flat tires in a single week in 1993. Coincidentally 5 of these flats happened within a half a mile of the next vulcanizadora on the highway. Odd how that happens...

Getting your vehicle serviced in Mexico is amazingly simple. In the United States we have become a disposable society. The cost of labor is so high that you can often buy something new cheaper than you have the old one fixed. In Mexico labor is literally dirt cheap. A good mechanic might make $35 or $40 per week. They still know how to fix things. My tire story above is one example. Here is one more story to illustrate my point.

On one trip to Mexico my van decided that it didn't want to start. Hermano Jose walked down the street to a local mechanic shop (Taller Mechanico) and made arrangements to have the vehicle repaired. The mechanic walked up to the hotel parking lot with a battery, jumper cables, and a few hand tools in a wheel barrow. After a few minutes he had the van running, but said the starter was bad and needed to be repaired. He put the wheel barrow in the back of the van, climbed into the driver's seat and motioned us to join him. My friends, until you have careened down the narrow side streets of a small Mexican town with a native at the wheel, you just haven't lived. In a matter of minutes he had my van pulled into his "shop" which consisted of 4 wooden posts with a tin roof. No walls, no doors; just a couple of work benches and piles of rusted junk everywhere. He crawled under the van and pulled the starter off in a matter of minutes. He then proceeded to pull the starter apart piece by piece and examine it. He carefully laid the parts on the work bench in the order in which he had taken them out. After examining several parts he showed me one and said, "This one is no good but I fix." He looked at several more, placing them on the bench then came to another one that he said was no good. This second bad part he pitched onto one of the piles of rusted junk. Digging through another pile of rusted junk he picked up a part and said that this one would work instead. Satisfied that he had examined everything, he took the first bad part and walked through a hole in the fence to the neighboring property, which was a welding shop. He welded a bead on the bad part, then ground the bead smooth again, bringing it back with the announcement that it would be good now. He reassembled the entire starter in just a few minutes and touched it with the jumper cables to show me that it worked. Within an hour of pulling my van into his shed, he had completely rebuilt the starter and made it functional. Just like with the tire, I know who has this van now and the starter is still on there seven years later and still turning the engine over every time. The best part of this story is that the mechanic had to charge me nearly $15 for these repairs. He apologized for how expensive it was but he explained that he had to pay the owner of the welding shop for use of that facility as well. (I gave the man $20 and made a friend for life.)

Taking minors

There are some that would vote against taking minors on a mission trip to an under developed country like Mexico. Once upon a time I would have agreed with that sentiment, but in the last few years I have seen too much good come from having young people see the needs of Mexico for themselves. Reading a book, watching a video or listening to a missionary talk will help you understand what it is like, but there is no substitute for experiencing it yourself. I mentioned a young lady named Katy in a previous chapter. She felt God calling her to participate in the Mexico missions but at that time the church missions committee was hesitant to allow teenagers to go without their parents. In this case, her mother, Dena, finally caved and made the trip with us. Today Katy, Dena, and another sibling are making plans to return to Ukraine where they have been working for several years now. I also mentioned our youngest daughter, Amanda, in a previous chapter. She made a couple of trips with us before her educational responsibilities prevented her return and she misses it dearly. Both of these young ladies came back from their first mission trip with a completely different attitude towards missions in general and the people of

Working in Mexico

Mexico. As is so often the case, we go down there to minister to somebody else only to have the Lord change our hearts in the process.

Our church now has a policy that children can go on mission trips with their parents in attendance or at age 16 with written parental permission from BOTH parents. This is important to note: To prevent one parent from fleeing to Mexico with the child during a custody battle, the written permission take the child to Mexico must be signed by both custodial parents. Even if one parent goes on the trip, you need written permission from the other parent.

If taking minors on a foreign mission trip without their parents, you should obtain power of attorney with specific permission to secure medical and surgical treatment in case of an emergency. Since I'm not a lawyer and don't want to provide legal advice I can't provide a copy of the forms we used, but I'll tell you that these things can be obtained relatively cheaply via software, internet, or if God is really providing for you, through a church member who happens to be a lawyer. However you get it done – get it done. Don't take a minor across the border without the ability to take care of them in time of need.

Keeping in touch

Use of the phone systems in Mexico can be tricky. Unlike many of the advertisements posted by the Mexican Tourism Ministry, we have yet to find an operator that spoke English. In general, what you need to do is to dial 00 to get an international line, then 1 which is the country code for the USA and then the area code and telephone number as normal. The problem is that most of the hotels where we stay are not used to international travelers and have access codes just to get an outside line, and since all of the instructions are in Spanish we had problems getting through.

You can easily have somebody back home call you at your hotel. From the U.S. you dial 011 to get an international line, then 52 which is the country code for Mexico, then the 3 digit city code and 7 digit phone number for your location in Mexico. This has worked well for us in the past.

Another easy way of staying in touch is to contact your cell phone service provide a couple of weeks before you plan to leave and have them authorize your phone for use in Mexico. Many U.S. cell phones are blocked from use in foreign countries to make it harder to steal them and sell them across the border so you have to let your service provider know that you are planning on traveling abroad, to where, and for how long.

The way we have always kept in touch while on the road is via the Internet. Some hotels offer free access from a computer in the lobby. Most towns have one or more Internet Cafés which is a cheap and easy way to get online. The charge to use a computer hooked up to the internet is around 10 pesos (less than one dollar) per hour. You can walk in, plop down your 10 peso coin, sign on to Yahoo or Hotmail and keep the field team in touch with the home team.

Money exchange issues

Along the border you can usually spend American Dollars just as easy as you can Mexican Pesos. Once you get into the interior you pretty much have to conduct business in Pesos. To accomplish this you will have to schedule time in your travel plans to allow your team to visit a Casa de Cambio (a money exchange house) somewhere along the border. Each member can convert their dollars to pesos at the window. Be careful to only convert what you really want to spend, because when you sell the pesos back to dollars at the end of the trip you lose a few bucks in the transition. These folks are in business to make money. There is a government imposed limit of $5,000 per person, which is WAY more than any one person needs on a week long trip. The only time we have pushed up against this limit is when we were taking large sums of money down for a construction project. In those few cases we split the money up amongst the travelers for the sake of converting it in smaller quantities. The rates vary by day and by year, but in the last few years the exchange rate has hovered around 10 to 12 pesos per dollar. Your budget will depend greatly upon where you go and where you stay, but we have typically made these trips for around $400 per person for a week long stay.

Personal and team supplies

Many of our mission trips have included cases of Bibles and hymnals; boxes full of VBS supplies, clothes, and other materials; all in addition to our personal items. At times we have also taken sound systems, guitars to use, guitars to donate, chairs, tables, and even a lawnmower. Here's the problem: Mexico limits the value of what you bring into the country to $300 per person. More than that – in their opinion – and you have to pay a value tax of 30% of what they believe the value of the materials to be. Not exactly extortion, but due to the variation in interpretation and application, this can be a hassle. If you can buy it in Mexico it makes it easier. They don't believe for a second that you are giving it all away. They assume you are selling it down there which takes money out of their economy. To cut down on problems during the various inspections, we have learned to pack as many of our supplies and materials as possible into suitcases, which get searched a lot less frequently than boxes. In our case we have been blessed to have a local ministry (H.I.S. Ministries) that was able and willing to donate dozens of suitcases when ever we were planning a trip. In your case you may need to ask your local congregation to loan you suitcases for the trip. Consider opening the case of Bibles and asking each team member to pack a couple of them into their suitcases. This makes it a lot

Working in Mexico

harder to catch as a full case of new materials. It will be worth the effort but you might as well get used to the inspections – they will happen either way.

If the border guards deem that you have too much material, you will have to inventory the stuff you are taking across and then pay the 30% tax. You don't have to like it, but you should be prepared to pay it. The last time I crossed the border we had six people in a single pickup truck with the bed of the truck piled level with stuff. The border guards didn't think too much of it but the local cops in the next little town decided we had too much stuff and spent 30 minutes trying to extract the tax themselves. These things happen. Just pray a lot and know that if God wants that stuff in Mexico He'll provide a way to make it happen.

We have found that the hotel maid service nearly everywhere we have traveled has been willing to help with laundry service. Sometimes this is through the hotel, sometimes through a cousin down the street. In Ciudad Mante at the Hotel Monterrey the maids will take your laundry from you in the morning when you leave for VBS and have it washed, dried, folded, and laying on your bed by the time you come back in the afternoon, and for just a couple of dollars per load. It is much easier to pack if you know you don't have to pack quite so much.

Now for a list of things that you should consider packing for your trips:

- Wash cloths – not standard issue in Mexican hotels so if you want one, take one. We usually pick up a bundle of cheapies from the dollar store and just leave them behind.

- Toilet paper – few rest rooms facilities in Mexico come complete with what we consider an essential item. Carry rolls in zip lock baggies to keep the paper clean and dry in transit. Because of the condition of the facilities in the stops we've made, we now carry a small camp toilet like you can find at Academy or Wal-Mart. If you have the space, you'll appreciate this idea some day. We even have portable changing room that works as a portable outhouse in an emergency.

- Lip balm and sun screen - You will find the conditions hot and dry in the summer time.

- Bug spray - The bugs are both plentiful and hungry. I'm even convinced that mosquitoes are partial to Type O because I get eaten up when nobody else notices them.

- Bottled water – It is not a problem to find bottled water in Mexico, but since we know we will need a lot of water for the drive as well as for the trip, we typically pick up a couple of cases before we go. Here's our rule: ***If you don't break the seal on the bottle you don't drink the water.*** We had known for a while that the bottled water was okay but to avoid the tap water. Seeing 5 gallon bottles of water in the hotel hallways, we drank our fill. The next morning when most of the team was too sick to get out of bed we see the hotel clerk out back re-filling the bottles from the garden hose. The water was in a bottle but was definitely not bottled water if you get my meaning. Tap water in Mexico contains micro-organisms that our bodies are not used to, resulting in severe gastrointestinal distress. The water is not unsafe to the locals, but hurts us. Interestingly enough, the one time that some of the guys from Mexico were able to visit us here in our home, our well water did not sit well on their stomachs. On a related topic, the restaurants wash the food in the tap water. If you eat the lettuce you also consume the tap water. Fruits than can be peeled (bananas, mangos, pineapples) are fine but fruits that are washed and eaten whole (apples, strawberries) are potentially hazardous to your health. We tend to avoid raw veggies when traveling through Mexico – not because of the veggies but because of the water they are washed in.

- Baby wipes and/or waterless hand cleaner – you will find many Mexican rest stops are missing the basics such as running water, soap, and paper towels.

- Sometimes we visit our local doctor before the trip and he prescribes Levaquin – an antibiotic that we can take daily while on the trip to stave off Montezuma's revenge. You'll have to talk to your doctor about this possibility.

- Finally, a well stocked first aid kit – don't leave the states without one. Some items that we would recommend carrying in such a kit include:
    - Anti diarrhea medications
    - Something for an upset stomach
    - Something for headaches
    - If you're doing construction work with a bunch of middle aged office workers, don't forget the backache medication
    - Eye drops
    - Band aids
    - Antiseptic
    - Antacids

Border crossing don'ts

Mexico does not allow you to carry firearms into the country without special permits. They don't even allow you to have ammunition in your vehicle. Some websites are saying the rules have been somewhat relaxed in recent years, but the published penalty for getting caught with an unauthorized weapon or ammunition is time in a Mexican prison.

It should go without saying, but we'll say it anyway. Carrying illegal drugs is a bad idea. If you get caught you are going to prison. In the United States a person is innocent until proven guilty. This is not the system in use in Mexico. There you are guilty until proven innocent and it is very difficult to prove your innocence when you're behind bars.

I asked one of the Federales if I could take his picture at a check point once. He said no. I raised my hand to my camera (strapped around my neck) and asked if just one picture would be okay. He raised his hands to the automatic weapon strapped around his neck and let me know in no uncertain terms that such an action would not be permitted. No joking around with guys that carry loaded automatic weapons. This picture was snapped through the back window of the van as we were driving off.

We've also had a few minor issues coming back into the United States. Ever since 9-11 security has been understandably tighter. The border checks are much more thorough and these guards also have very little patience for joking around. You cannot bring back any kind of fruit that contains a seed. They even confiscated my sugar cane. No animals, no soil. Some people buy prescription drugs in Mexico because you can get them cheap and without a prescription. Interstate shipment (including importation) of unapproved drugs is prohibited by U.S. law. This includes foreign made versions of U.S. approved drugs. If you do bring back prescription drugs from Mexico you are supposed to have a valid prescription from a U.S. doctor with you and you are supposed to declare the drugs to U.S. Customs. Customs will allow "reasonable" amounts of medications for personal use but no stockpiling or purchasing of large amounts for resale or any commercial use.

Chapter 11: Cultural tips

This chapter is intended to capture some of our cultural learnings from our mission experiences in Mexico.

First off: Partner with someone who not only speaks the language fluently but also is familiar with the culture. I've mentioned this already but it bears repeating. Speaking Spanish is not the same as being able to communicate effectively. There are cultural differences that can cause you serious problems if you don't understand how to work with the Mexican people. My recommendation is that you work with a local partner – perhaps a local Hispanic congregation – that in turn works with a mission partner on site in Mexico. Over the years our local partner has been Primera Iglésia Bautista in Dickinson, Texas. Often times they desired to accomplish something of lasting meaning in Mexico but struggled with the resources as their congregation is small. By partnering with a larger church we were able to accomplish a lot more together than either of our congregation could have by ourselves. They brought a knowledge and understanding of how to work in the Mexican culture as well as language expertise. We brought teams of people that did not understand the culture but had resources available to help out. I cannot over emphasize this point.

While the last few years has not made us experts in Mexican culture, we have picked up a few things that you might find interesting as well as helpful in your own mission efforts. When we say we are going to the church, we mean we are going to the church building, even though most of us know that the church is not a building, the church is the body of believers. We just use the word church to mean both the building and the body of believers depending on the context. In Spanish they use two different words. The word *iglésia* is translated as church but means the body of believers. The word *templo* is translated as temple and means the building where the body of believers meet to worship. When you talk to people in Mexico you would not say that you are going to drive down to the church (*iglésia*) as this would not make sense to them. You would say you are going to drive down to the *templo* instead. We did not build a church (*iglésia*) in Faja de Oro, we helped to build a temple for the church.

If you took Spanish in High School or college (like we did) then you were taught that you greet people with the word "*Hola!*" meaning hello. In nearly 15 years of mission work in Mexico I have never once had a Mexican greet me with the word *hola*. In the morning you are greeted with "*buenas días*" which means good day or good morning. In the afternoon they would say "*buenas tardes* – good afternoon. After sundown the greeting would be "buenas noches" or good evening. This is how you are greeted and how you should greet others in secular meetings in Mexico.

While the above is still technically true when greeting the brethren in spiritual settings, there is a little more to the story. The only way the folks in the church greet each other is with the phrase "Dios le bendiga" which means God Bless You. They use this same phrase when saying goodbye. (They do not use this phrase when you sneeze . . .) When you meet somebody upon entering the temple or meet somebody whom you know to be part of the body of believers out on the street you may say God Bless You first or maybe they will. You can respond with the same phrase or the response might be "*igualmente*" which literally means equally to you.

Another difference between secular and spiritual Mexico is the use of titles. In school we learned that you call men Señor and ladies Señora or Señorita which is equivalent to the use of mister, missus, and miss in English respectively. In your secular dealings in Mexico this is perfectly correct. When greeting or conversing with people in the church, you are expected to recognize the family ties. We are all part of the family of God and that makes us all brothers and sisters. In Mexico everybody in the church (the body of believers) refers to each other as *Hermano* or *Hermana* – brother or sister. In Mexico I'm not Mr. Lamar or Mr. Jim, I'm Hermano Jim. To address my dear friend and coworker in Faja de Oro as Goyo without a title would be inappropriate. Señor Goyo would be correct but very formal. This would be appropriate for business meetings but not within the family of God. In their eyes I would be ignoring or even worse - denying the family tie. I must always call him Hermano Goyo – Brother Goyo – so that every time we speak we reaffirm that we are brothers in Christ. In the work of the church, you can even just address people as Hermano or Hermana if you can't remember their names. We have found that this cultural difference carries over into the English language when working with Hispanics in the United States. Even if we are speaking English they always refer to us as Brother Jim and Sister Carol.

Mexico is still very much a male dominated society. Women on the mission team need to understand that a domineering attitude will alienate the men and women that they are trying to minister to. When it comes time to talk business, the Mexican women excuse themselves. I'm not defending their attitude or condoning it - just telling it like it is. The concept of machismo extends to more than just sexism. In general the Mexican people are very mild mannered

Cultural Tips

and very respectful towards each other. Mexicans in authority do not accept public criticism or challenge very well – from men or women. To confront a pastor or deacon in the church down there is extremely insulting – even if the confrontation is a relatively simple question with no intent to be insulting. Authority is to be respected at all costs. If you have a question about something strategic, take the authority figure aside and ask the question in a very non-threatening and non-personal manner. Otherwise you run the risk of alienating the very people with whom you need a strong working relationship in order to succeed.

In this, and many other ways, Mexico is about 50 years behind our times. A large percentage of their population still lives in rural areas with outhouses for facilities. They still wash clothes on rub-boards and hang the laundry out to dry. If they have money they might own a ringer washing machine which is still available in stores as new equipment in Mexico. In short, they live a lot like my grandparents lived 40 to 50 years ago.

Good social manners are important in Mexico. When you first meet somebody new in Mexico you are expected to greet them. When you enter the temple you are expected to greet everybody already there. When somebody else comes in you can expect that they will make the rounds to greet everybody there. Walking in and sitting down without greeting them is deemed as rude. They teach this to their children so well that we routinely have little 5 and 6 year olds coming up to us to shake our hands and welcome us. Within the dealing of the church, hugging is as common as shaking hands once they have gotten to know you. Remember, once they know you in the spiritual sense you are now part of the family.

Let's talk about time. Punctuality is not near as important to the Mexicans as it is to us. Things are scheduled to start at a certain time, but actually start whenever it seems appropriate to start. Maybe thirty minutes after the scheduled start time, maybe more. We have gone to church services where there were only five or six people there when it was time to start. An hour later there were over fifty people gathered for services. Some of this is just a difference in attitude and some it refers back to the importance of social manners. If they were visiting with somebody else at 5:59 PM they would NEVER tell that person that they had somewhere else to be at 6:00 PM so they must be excused. Out of respect for the person they were already visiting with they would stay and visit until that person left, then they would go to church. Because of this difference in how important we perceive time to be, it is extremely common to have people showing up for services after the service has started, even when you start late. Don't get offended if they aren't there on time. It is just part of who they are.

In addition to not starting on time, they rarely if ever finish on time. One reason for this is obvious. If you start late you are most likely going to finish late as well. Another reason for this is a little less obvious. The people of Mexico do not have a preconceived notion that church services should last no longer than 60 minutes and should include 3 songs, an offering, special music, and a sermon with an invitation not to exceed 3 versus of Just As I Am. They come to worship and worship they will. Given the chance to offer a word of testimony, you might have 5 or 10 people step forward to tell how the Lord has blessed them or to request prayer for an issue that they are facing. When asked if anybody has a song or special music to share you might have one person step forward or you might have 4 or 5 people step up. Impromptu choirs are formed at the drop of a hat. Somebody may ask to sing a song and then sing 3 songs. When the preacher gets going he will feel no compunction to finish until he's through. Personally I like that approach. I think preachers ought to deliver the message that God gave them no matter how much or little time that takes. All these things taken together means a church service may easily last a couple of hours.

Getting invited into somebody's home is a special privilege. This will only occur after becoming personal friends and establishing trust. It is a great honor to be invited into their homes. Having a gift for the host and hostess is an excellent idea. Nothing elaborate, just something to show that you appreciate the gesture. On our GBA recon trip in February of 2003 I was surprised to be invited to stay in the home of Hermano Julian with Kyle Cox. Our first evening there Kyle presented the Luna's with a wrapped present – a little picture book about Texas. I asked him about this later and he said he too was surprised by this specific invitation, but that he had learned long ago never to go unprepared for this type of eventuality. I have never traveled back to Mexico without a gift or two in my luggage since then.

Hospitality is important to the Mexican people, regardless of their station in life, especially in the church. You are taking supplies and expending considerable effort to make these trips. They are grateful. They desire to reciprocate and you must let them. On one trip Hermano Goyo invited the entire mission team to visit with his family in their front yard. They cut up cantaloupe into bite sized squares, stuck toothpicks in the pieces and served them to the group on a paper plate graciously sharing what they had with us. On our last trip the father of the lady who lives on the hill above the proposed new church site slaughtered one of his two pigs and cooked it for us so that the entire

Cultural Tips

congregation could share a fellowship meal. They shared what they had and we were moved by their generosity. One more lesson that you might take away from this topic is to gratefully eat what they provide as it may in fact represent a huge sacrifice on their part. Leaving the last couple of bites on your plate is a good way of letting your host know that they have provided plenty for you. Cleaning your plate may insinuate that your host was unable to provide all that you desired.

These people are your Christian brothers and sisters. As long you are trying, they are very loving and very forgiving, so don't let this chapter scare you. These hints are just provided to help you fit in as easily as possible.

Chapter 12: Summary and conclusions

So let's take just a few pages to reflect. What have we learned so far?

- ✞ The Lord already knows how to do what He wants done. You don't have to understand it when you start. Just do what He wants and trust God to take care of the rest.
- ✞ The seed you plant today may take a while to germinate and grow. Just plant the seeds and trust God to take care of the rest.
- ✞ There are no small jobs in God's kingdom. What seems small to you may be just what He needs to get the job done. Just do what He says and trust God to take care of the rest.
- ✞ You don't need to start a new work. Just join God where you see Him already at work.
- ✞ Don't expect God to make it easy for you. Learn to experience joy in serving Him even when things aren't going your way. James 1: 2-4
- ✞ A little suffering for the Lord is to be expected. Praise Him for the privilege. 1 Peter 4: 12-19
- ✞ God has a plan. He may share it with you. He may not. The work is His. Just go and do what He tells you to do and trust Him to take care of the rest.
- ✞ You can't out give God. He'll use whatever you provide to further His kingdom, maybe in ways you never dreamed of. Just give and trust Him to take care of the rest.
- ✞ You have to be flexible. You can plan and study all you want, but in the end you have to go where God sends you and do as He bids.
- ✞ While working diligently to minister to others, don't forget to take time to recharge your own batteries.
- ✞ A little bit goes a long way in the hands of the Lord. Don't hold back because you don't think you have enough. Just give and trust God to multiply your offering.
- ✞ As you go, spread the word. Long distance mission trips are great, but we were commanded to spread the good news in our home town as well as the uttermost parts of the world.
- ✞ Missions is not a spectator sport. Go prepared to do something. Be prepared to work, sing, speak, or make funny faces if that what God calls you to do. 2 Timothy 4:2

We have seen a lot of seeds planted. We've watered and we've fertilized. We have been blessed to see a bountiful harvest from some of these efforts. We have also been blessed to watch folks get excited about missions through some of these efforts. Someday, on this side or the other side of the Jordan I expect to hear how Feliz has been working for the Lord with her guitar. In the years to come I expect I'll see at least some of the fruits that are yielded because of the efforts of Katy, Amanda, and Sulema. The lives that they touch will in turn touch other lives as the Word of God ripples across the planet.

The harvest is truly plentiful and the workers truly few. Is God calling you to the harvest? I believe He is. I believe He calls each and every one of us to be harvesters. In the great commission Jesus told us all to "Go ye therefore . . ." Matt 28:19. In Acts 1:8 He further clarifies this message by telling us that we will be His witnesses and directs us to tell the world about Him starting in our own home towns, then our states, then our countries, and finally spreading the good news to the uttermost parts of the world. You may not be called to Mexico, but you are called to missions. Your mission may be next door or down the street. Your mission may be in a neighboring community or neighboring state. But make no mistake, you are called to missions. Maybe your role in foreign missions is to be part of the home team instead of the field team. That's a wonderful position. The field teams need prayer and fiscal support in order to accomplish what God calls us to do.

Jesus commands us all to go. I exhort you to obey His command. In my experience the more you give of yourself the richer you become.

When you come back, share your experiences with your church body. Some go far away. Some stay closer to home. Some give. Some pray. Each member of the body plays a different role in the effort. It is important for the field team to share their experiences with the home team so that everybody on the team can be blessed by the effort.

Then share your experiences with other church bodies. It may be that there are others seeking God's will that would love to be a part of the effort. Go forth and multiply.

In order to put these words into actions I leave you with this final offer:

Carol and I would love to share our missions experiences with you personally and we make ourselves available to you and your church. We would also love to hear about your mission experiences so that the body of Christ may be lifted up and encouraged by each other. Please feel free to drop me a note at Jim_Lamar@yahoo.com. We look forward to working together to spread the good news of Jesus Christ to a lost and dying world.

www.ingramcontent.com/pod-product-compliance
Lightning Source LLC
Chambersburg PA
CBHW022305060426
42446CB00007BA/593